CHARTER MARK

Awarded for excellence

Kent
County
Council

Born in London, Charlotte Uhlenbroek spent her early life in Nepal. She studied Zoology and Psychology at Bristol University, then spent four years living in Gombe National Park in Tanzania, studying chimpanzees for her PhD in Zoology. She has presented a number of programmes for the BBC, including the acclaimed *Cousins* and *Talking with Animals*.

JUNGLE

For zoologist Charlotte Uhlenbroek, being
besieged by ants or dangled from a balloon
high above the rainforest is all in a day's
work. In making her new BBC TV series,
Jungle, she had to deal with all this and more.
Using the latest technology, Charlotte was
able to explore the tree canopy in Borneo
— a landscape hundreds of feet off the
ground. Among her other challenges were a
boat trip through the flooded forest of the
Amazon, where pink dolphins swim, and a
journey through the dense jungle of the
Congo, last refuge of the gorillas. In the
tradition of David Attenborough and Gerald
Durrell, Charlotte describes her experiences.

CHARLOTTE UHLENBROEK

JUNGLE

Complete and Unabridged

CHARNWOOD
Leicester

First published in Great Britain in 2003 by
Hodder & Stoughton
a division of Hodder Headline, London

By arrangement with the BBC
The BBC logo is a registered trademark of the
British Broadcasting Corporation
and is used under licence. BBC logo © 1996

First Charnwood Edition
published 2005
by arrangement with
Hodder & Stoughton
a division of Hodder Headline, London

British Library CIP Data

Uhlenbroek, Charlotte
 Jungle.—Large print ed.—
 Charnwood library series
 1. Uhlenbroek, Charlotte—Travel
 2. Rain forest ecology 3. Rain forest plants
 4. Jungle animals 5. Rain forest animals
 6. Jungle ecology 7. Large type books
 I. Title
 577.3′4

 ISBN 1–84395–686–1

Published by
F. A. Thorpe (Publishing)
Anstey, Leicestershire
Set by Words & Graphics Ltd.
Anstey, Leicestershire
Printed and bound in Great Britain by
T. J. International Ltd., Padstow, Cornwall

This book is printed on acid-free paper

For my beloved Dan, Fran and Marijke

Contents

1

Exploring the Last Frontier

As dawn seeped into the sky we spread out the silky blue material of the balloon in a large clearing in the forest. We were in Sabah in Borneo. The air was heavy with a damp mist and it was quiet except for an eerily beautiful song that floated through the jungle: a melodious series of bubbling notes, like water and a woodwind instrument combined, gradually building in pitch and volume and ending as a cascading trill. It was a pair of gibbons singing a duet to reaffirm the bond between them and lay claim to a nearby patch of the forest.

Laurent yanked on the cord to start the two-stroke engine but it gave a desultory cough and died. He yanked it again. And again. It reminded me of endless battles at home with the lawn-mower. 'Ah, *zut!*' he said, throwing up his arms in exasperation. After a couple more tugs, the engine spluttered into life and a polished-wood propeller whirred into action. We were setting up a motorised hot-air balloon, a *cinebulle*; it had been brought to Borneo by two Frenchmen called Dany and Laurent and would allow us to explore the rainforest canopy. Dany was the cinebulle pilot, a quiet man, while Laurent was boisterous and expansive. In his own words, he was 'someone who gets to play with lots of toys'.

The film crew were gathered round, yawning and drinking coffee from a thermos while helping to set up the balloon. A couple of us held the mouth wide and while Laurent directed the blast of air from the propeller into it, Dany walked round straightening the fabric envelope as it filled out, then attached a last bit of material to cap the top. Peering down the inside of the envelope as it is being inflated feels like looking into a giant billowing blue tent.

The cinebulle could only take two people, one of whom would be the pilot. I was going with Dany on this flight and we had rigged it with video cameras; Si, our cameraman, would go on a separate flight to do aerials. As soon as the envelope was full of air, Dany opened the valve of the propane cylinder, fired up the burner and sent in a jet of flame to heat it. Gradually the balloon rose until it was vertical. Dany told me to sit on the seat to weigh it down, made a few final checks then sat next to me. We were ready to go.

We lifted gently off the ground and the figures

below us shrank to doll-size. Looking down as we passed high over the coffee-brown river, my legs dangling, I felt a bit apprehensive. Then we were rising above the trees, skimming the canopy, floating higher and higher. Riveted by the view I forgot my fear and leaned out, straining on my seat-belt to see all I could of this new realm, the rainforest canopy: the last frontier on earth to be explored.

Rainforest encircles the globe in a broken band of green along the equator from South America through Africa to South East Asia. It covers just 6 per cent of the land surface of the planet, but contains more than half of all known animal and plant species. They provide us with a host of medicines, materials and everyday foods, from coffee and bananas, to chocolate and ginger. But forests are much more than a list of the plants and animals that live there: what makes them exceptional is the complex network of relationships that exist between the innumerable species. The rainforest is more like a giant organism and to understand it we have to understand food webs, dispersal systems and the interdependence of the plants and animals that live there.

The trees are central to this world: they dominate life in the jungle, making up 97 per cent of all living matter. They are the tallest form of life on earth and, when viewed from above, their crowns form a continuous rolling green land. The canopy is the driving force behind the whole forest system yet until the last few years it has been all but beyond our reach. Now, at last, it is open for investigation, and Borneo, which boasts some of the tallest trees in the world, seemed a pretty good place to start.

The cinebulle grazed the tree-tops. 'It's good up here, no?' Dany said, laughing at my huge grin.

It was awesome. The forest around us was indistinct and shrouded in mist, the trees appearing as giant phantoms, their smooth and sculpted branches reaching out like open arms.

We set a course south-east towards the sun, a bright disc just visible through the haze. As we gained height the forest below us faded and for a time we were enveloped in mist. Dany and I said little to each other as, intermittently, the burner fired up behind our heads with a loud roar that made conversation difficult. But it didn't matter — all that we wanted to express could easily be done with an exchange of jubilant smiles. Anyway, he had to concentrate — we were flying through fog with no instruments to guide us.

Suddenly, out of nowhere, a tree of colossal proportions loomed up before us. The average height of the canopy is a considerable 45 metres but a few trees — known as 'emergents' — simply dwarf the rest of the forest, standing nearly double that at 75–80 metres. It was a Mengarris, a huge, pale-limbed giant rising clear above the rest, its feathery crown isolated like a tufted island in the ocean of mist.

Head and shoulders above the rest, emergents, like the Mengarris and the taller Dipterocarp trees, experience an entirely different environment from those that crowd together in the canopy about their midriffs. Above the canopy, they are open to the more violent forces of nature and have to be tough. They commonly lose branches to fierce tropical rainstorms or high winds, and are regularly struck by lightning. At other times searing sun and warm winds strip them of water.

There are benefits, though, to being so tall. These massive trees don't have to compete for sunlight, their leaves are out of the reach of most leaf-eating mammals and insects, and they have almost exclusive use of the tropical breeze that continuously moves over the canopy, carrying their winged or fluffy seeds for miles over the forest. In many parts of Borneo there are stands of emergents, which raise the entire canopy by about 30 metres. This, of course, cancels out all the benefits of the emergent lifestyle: a group of Borneo's tree species are engaged in an active 'arms race' to the skies, each species trying to outgrow the next; it has led to the formation of the tallest tropical rainforests in the world. But there is a limit to their size. Our earth's surface is covered by a relatively thin mantle of life; even trees, the tallest of all life forms, rarely reach more than 100 metres because their growth is constrained by gravity.

When the mist started to burn off, low, forest-clad hills took shape in the distance. The air cleared rapidly, leaving just a few fragile wisps, and the trees below us glowed in the morning light. Dany steered us expertly over them, intermittently firing up the burner behind our heads. A roar accompanied by a blast of heat

5

lifted the hot-air balloon — a cheerful blue, red, white and yellow orb sailing over a sea of green.

As I looked out over the forest I was staggered by the variety of trees: some two thousand species are found here, and even a 25-acre patch supports more different types than the entire United States. But they have one vital characteristic in common: they harness the energy of the sun — and this time of day, the early morning, when the sun's warmth gains intensity, is the moment they are waiting for.

'Can we get a bit closer to that one?' I asked, pointing to a large fig below us.

It was going to test Dany's piloting skills. The air was warmer now and we were being carried by air currents that made it hard to control the cinebulle's movements precisely. We made the first pass too high. 'One moment,' Dany said, and circled to try again. This time we crashed into the top of the tree. Dany grabbed a branch with his feet to stop us floating away while I caught a leaf — it was smallish and unremarkable, but this humble bit of cellulose is responsible for the most important chemical reaction on the planet: 'making with light', or photosynthesis. Virtually all life depends on it. Animals (including ourselves) cannot make their own food: everything we eat — whether it is plants or other animals that have eaten plants, is ultimately a product of photosynthesis.

Now that the mist had cleared we could feel the strength of the sun on our arms and faces. Below us, the innumerable leaves that cover every tree were acting like tiny solar panels capturing its energy. As the rays strike each leaf and are absorbed by chlorophyll, it takes in only the blue and red wavelengths, while green and yellow light is simply reflected. This is why plants are green — we 'see' the colour that an object reflects. The energy from the blue and red light splits the water that plants take up through their roots into oxygen and hydrogen. This releases a burst of energy, which the plant then uses to make carbohydrates by combining the newly released hydrogen with carbon dioxide absorbed from the air.

Photosynthesis goes on in plants all over the globe, but in the tropics it happens on a massive scale. Below me the greatest powerhouse on earth, a giant solar factory, was soaking up sunshine and turning it into energy for living systems. The world's rainforests produce something in the region of 20 million megawatts of power, enough to fuel two thousand New Yorks and enough to power an astonishing variety of life. When I first learned about photosynthesis at school, my biology teacher, Mr Davis, impressed upon my class its importance to life on earth. He told us that if we ever discovered how to re-create the process artificially, we'd solve the world's energy problems at a stroke.

It is clear that everything about the rainforest trees is geared to trapping sunlight. They climb towards the sun, their trunks growing straight up; at the top their branches spread wide to catch the rays with every leaf. This is the ultimate in sun worship and there is no better place for it than the tropics, the intensity of light is far greater than it is in temperate zones: at the equator, sunbeams strike the earth perpendicularly rather than obliquely, focusing the energy on a smaller area. Moreover, the equator doesn't tilt appreciably towards and away from the sun during the year so the light is unchanging, with day length and temperature more or less constant.

But this amount of light can be too much even for the trees. The ultra-violet rays can damage leaves, just as Dany and I could feel it burning our skin. At midday in the tropics the sun is particularly ferocious, which may be why the leaves of the tallest trees tended to be small and many were angled to catch the less harmful rays of early morning and late afternoon.

Below us a pair of hornbills flew over the rolling green landscape of tree-tops, their wing-beats heavy in the warm air. Every tree was unique — some were smooth-limbed, while others supported flourishing gardens in their branches. Giant bushy ferns, with fronds shaped like antlers, balanced on top of wide branches or pendulous, antler-shaped fronds of the beautiful stag-horn ferns hanging down. Here and there I caught sight of exquisite white orchids or the deep red of new leaves. Dany pointed to a dark mound among the shadows created by the branches of a magnificent specimen, a huge teardrop-shaped honey-bees' nest. We decided that was one tree it was better not to investigate too closely.

With this kind of overview you begin to see patterns in the forest below. In temperate

8

woodlands, the boundary between the crowns of two trees is often marked by a zone of broken twigs and damaged buds, caused when they rub together in the wind. However, here the crowns of neighbouring trees are naturally separated by a gap of perhaps 50cm, a phenomenon charmingly known as 'crown shyness'. There are several theories why tropical trees should like to maintain their personal space, some have suggested that it is to stop leaf-eating animals such as caterpillars moving from tree to tree. An alternative is that it makes trees less vulnerable to being toppled by others in the raging storms of the tropics.

We had travelled some distance and I realised how valuable the cinebulle is for surveying the forest. On the ground, it would have taken days to cover the same distance through the undergrowth but up here we could not only move quickly but our bird's eye view enabled us to appreciate the number of different trees, discover which were in flower or fruiting, and which had occupants, such as bees or nesting birds of prey. However, the balloon can be used only when there is little wind, which restricts flights to the first couple of hours after dawn when the air is still.

The wind was already picking up and it was time to return to base. As we approached the engine started to sputter, threatening to cut out. I glanced at Dany, who muttered something I didn't catch and repeatedly pushed the red ignition button. He seemed more annoyed than worried. Since 1975 Dany has flown hot-air balloons all over the world — he made the first solo flight over Mont Blanc — and had encountered worse problems. The wind up here was getting stronger by the minute though, and if the engine cut it would be hard to control where we went. Without an engine who knew where we could end up — in a forest stretching for tens of miles in every direction finding somewhere to land would be difficult. With a bit more coughing and spluttering the engine limped on until we saw the Danum Valley Research Centre clearing below us, and were soon back on the ground. It had been a spectacular flight — a great way to begin my rainforest odyssey.

We had arrived at the research centre a few days before. Scott, the film's director, Jake, the sound recordist, and I had flown in from Kota Kinabalu, the capital of Sabah province in Malaysian Borneo, to Lahad Datu, a small bustling town on the coast. As we stepped out of the air-conditioned plane and walked down the steps, the wall of heat practically brought us to a standstill. In November the temperature is around 35° Celsius, and the humidity can be as much as 99 per cent. It was as much as we could do to collect our baggage in the chaotic one-roomed airport building and drag it to the Nissan pick-up that would take us on to join the rest of the crew.

The road led inland and we passed small wooden houses perched on low stilts, their verandas crowded with colourful hanging baskets and dogs sprawled in the shade. Gradually the houses thinned and the coconut palms, cassava and banana trees that surrounded them gave way to gentle, verdant slopes. We left the main road and turned on to a bumpy track that led into the forest. Immediately the atmosphere changed. Dense vegetation pressed in on us from both sides in an impenetrable tangle — thickets of low shrubs and bushes fought for space, saplings struggled towards the light, twisted lianas clung to the trees. Beyond, nothing was visible but dark shadows.

Every now and then a hillock would stand proud of the forest or the land would dip steeply away from the road, providing a window on to our surroundings. The forest of Borneo is a botanical paradise and home to monkeys, elephants, rhino, tapir, deer, antelope, sun bears, wild pigs, gibbons, orang-utans, and clouded leopards. Its natural wealth is largely down to Borneo's unusual history. It was an archipelago of islands until about five million years ago when the seabed buckled, due to tectonic activity, and the islands merged to form a sizeable land mass uniting an array of different wildlife. Then in the last two million years a series of ice ages have lowered the sea level as many as 20 times, creating temporary land bridges between Borneo, Sumatra, Java and mainland Asia, allowing successive waves of animals to make the trip across from the mainland before it was cut off again by the sea. About ten thousand years ago the sea rose for the last time, creating the current coastline of Borneo and isolating its residents on the third largest island in the world.

In the road ahead large piles of fresh dung told us that elephants had passed that way recently and I hoped we might encounter them on the other side of each bend. It was just as well that we didn't: Melvin, our enthusiastic young Malaysian driver, was intent on driving at bone-jarring speed over the rough road — as we careered round one corner we nearly ran straight into a large family of bearded pigs. A buff-coloured sow was leading six largish piglets across the road. As we screeched to a halt she stopped and stared at us, her moustache of upward-pointing bristles twitching beside her long fleshy snout. She appeared more indignant than frightened, but eventually hurried her family in to the safety of the undergrowth. We watched them until the last piglet had disappeared into the bushes, then Melvin gunned the engine and we drove on.

'Please slow down,' Scott asked him once, pushing back his long hair, which was blowing wildly around his face.

'Yes, I go slowly,' Melvin said, with a bright smile, and eased off the accelerator.

But he couldn't contain himself and minutes later he had floored it again, leaving a cloud of dust billowing behind us. We were concerned about the wildlife — and the condition of our vertebrae — but another danger lurked that we weren't aware of. As we came round another corner, Melvin slammed on the brakes and veered to the edge of the road. He had just missed the massive truck hurtling towards us. As it roared past its mission became apparent: piled high on the back were some two dozen vast logs.

The forest we were in was part of a huge logging concession. Despite its lush appearance and the presence of some impressive trees, most of it was secondary, or regrowth forest, which had been selectively logged twenty-five years ago and was now being relogged. Lowland rainforest once covered most of Borneo but huge tracts have been destroyed. What remains is in the south, in Indonesian Kalimantan, and in the north-east, in Malaysian Sabah. In Sabah, the largest rainforest areas occur between two great rivers, the Segama and the Kinabatangan, extending north to Sandakan Bay. Danum Valley Research Centre is located in the heart of this region on the Segama river, but even here the conservation area of 438 square kilometres is surrounded by forest that is being felled. Another logging truck roared past.

Forest that has been selectively logged looks quite different from primary rainforest: it has a much thicker understorey and a few species predominate. Macaranga trees, which are related to rubber trees, lined the road. There are over 250 species of Macaranga, and they are probably the most important pioneer species in South East Asia. They have an amazing capacity to appear as if by magic in freshly logged areas because they maintain a bank of dormant seeds deep in the soil of mature forest, ready and primed to burst into life should the canopy open up. Like all pioneer specialists, they are able to grow at an amazing rate. They channel all their

13

energy into vertical growth: their trunks are slender and pole-like and their leaves large. Like many successful plants they also employ animals to help them, and Macaranga trees have developed a remarkable relationship with ants. Because trees lack mobility they are unable to escape from danger and often have to endure attacks from hungry herbivores — so who better than to form a partnership with than a highly mobile and well-disciplined army? Cecropias go to great lengths to attract ants by producing special 'food bodies', like corpuscles that are packed with carbohydrates, some proteins and fats, like goody bags that the ants use to feed their queen and larvae. In addition, the trees provide shelter for the ants in the form of swollen stems with spaces suitable for nest sites. The ants that take up residence in these serviced apartments are Crematogaster ants — small, brown ants, 3–4 millimetres in length, named for their distinctive heart-shaped 'gaster' or rump. In Malay they are called *semut tonggek* which apparently refers to their habit of waving their gasters in the air when alarmed.

In return for food and shelter the ants' job is to protect their hosts from attack, sensing movement and swarming to see off any animal that tries to eat its leaves. If the ants sense movement of the tree that suggests that a herbivore may be eating its leaves, they instantly swarm and attack the animal, while vines trying to use the Macaranga for support find that any tendrils attempting to cling to the tree are bitten off by the ants. The ants seem to know, however, not to bite off any new shoots that belong to the tree itself.

Having ant security guards would appear to be of great benefit to trees and in turn, the success of these trees is essential to the regeneration of the forest. The pioneer species pave the way for the great hardwoods, and true rainforest is eventually established once more, but this can take more than a century. Beneath the Macaranga trees, a scrubby growth of dust-covered herbaceous plants was dominated by torch ginger. It has leafy shoots that grow taller than a man, and showy red flowers that bloom like blazing torches — the petals are a key ingredient in some fiery local dishes.

Danum Valley Research Centre was much grander than I had expected. There were several buildings, the largest comprising a library, laboratory and drying room, another a work-shop, small shop and laundry room, a third, a restaurant with a wide veranda, and there were various accommodation blocks, simple but well maintained and clean. The field centre was built for research, conservation and education. Several students study various aspects of forest ecology there, while residents of Lahad Datu often visit at weekends. It didn't feel as wild or remote as I had hoped, but it was the perfect headquarters from which to explore the forest.

We had a huge crew by natural history filming standards. In addition to Laurent, Dany, Si, Jake, Scott and myself, there was Karen, the series producer, Rita, the production co-ordinator, James and Andy, tree-climbing experts, Ced, our fixer, and our field assistant John. We also had a fair amount of equipment. Over breakfast we discussed logistics for the days to come. That morning James and Andy would rig trees with ropes while Dany and Laurent repaired the cinebulle engine and the rest of the crew filmed some sequences in the forest. That afternoon I would go up in the helium bubble.

With the schedule decided we helped ourselves to more eggs and toast. 'Toast? Another egg?', someone said offering the plate. 'Just toast please', Laurent replied helping himself. James deemed it was at last a fitting moment to tell his terrible egg joke. 'Okay' James said 'Here's one for you. Why do Frenchmen only have one egg for breakfast? . . . Because one egg is an oeuf!' Laurent nodded slowly munching his toast. 'Okay tell me why you English like this marmite for breakfast . . . 'We were already one big happy family.

Dany and Laurent are part of a team that includes Francis Halle, a botanist at the University of Montpellier in France. Halle decided that the best way to reach the canopy was from above, using a hot-air balloon. While the cinebulle is great for surveying the forest you can only fly at dawn and it's hard to stop at a particular tree for a closer look. In 1989, he had teamed up with Dany and Gilles Ebersolt, an architect, to find a radical new way of exploring the canopy.

They came up with several innovative ideas, the most exciting a huge raft, some 600 square metres in area, shaped like a spider's web (or, in

16

the latest version, a giant pretzel), which rests on top of the canopy. The main supporting struts are like sausages made from the same material as a Zodiac inflatable dinghy. A net, which allows you either to scramble about or to sleep, is stretched between them. It is transported to its location by airship and, if necessary, anchored to the branches with ropes. It will remain *in situ* for anything from ten days to two months. Scientists climb up to it on a rope that dangles to the ground. Rafts have been set up in forests around the world — in Gabon, Cameroon, Madagascar and Guyana — and researchers flock to join the expeditions, which have reaffirmed the importance of the band of green that encircles the globe. For instance, from access to the canopy, scientists have started to make accurate measurements of the amount of carbon dioxide absorbed by rainforests. One such project, called the 'carbon sniffing project', compares the amount of carbon dioxide that is taken up by trees with what is released into the atmosphere through respiration, in order to discover how much carbon is sequestered by a forest.

Trees can take up five tonnes of carbon per hectare per year. There are 1.7 billion hectares of rainforest left so at this rate it is 8.5 billion tonnes a year. More than our total carbon emissions which is just under 6 billion tonnes a year. While forests also release carbon dioxide it still means that rainforests act as a huge carbon sink. The destruction of the forest through major forest fires such as the devastating fires that swept through Borneo in 1997 and 1998, and still continue to occur there from time to time, reduces the amount of carbon dioxide removed from the atmosphere and also releases vast quantities into the atmosphere, contributing to global warming. Another project is looking at the topography or 'surface roughness' of the canopy: the rougher the surface, the more water the trees release into the air, which contributes to rainfall.

Trees influence the environment and are in turn influenced by it. Recently some intriguing research has shown how their growing patterns are sensitive to their environment.

Finally, exploring the canopy has allowed us to discover what lives up there and to understand better how the resident monkeys, bats, birds and insects all play a vital role in the ecology of the forest.

I would have loved to explore the canopy from something resembling a bouncy castle, but it was too difficult and expensive for us to set up the raft for our short expedition in the forest. Instead, we had the bubble, a helium balloon with a small seat dangling below it. It had been developed by the same French team as the cinebulle, and is a simple, effective device that gives scientists unparalleled freedom to travel through the uppermost branches of the canopy making observations, collecting samples or setting insect traps. The balloon measures 210 cubic metres (it is about 7.5 metres in diameter). It is filled with helium, then weighted with water to achieve neutral buoyancy: it neither rises nor sinks but hangs mid-air. From a helicopter, we laid about a kilometre of rope over the canopy. A couple of slings run from the chair of the balloon and are clipped to the rope with two karabiners — oval-shaped steel rings with hinged gates. The rope slides through the karabiners, so you can pull yourself and the bubble along it to move through the canopy. Second and third ropes can be crossed with the first to create a network of routes and extend the balloon's range.

I wasn't too keen on going up in the bubble — I'm scared of heights and it looked a little unstable. Also, once I was up in it, I would be on my own if anything went wrong. 'Nothing will go wrong,' Laurent said, and patted my shoulder. 'It's wonderful, it's like flying!' He skipped forward, flinging his arms wide. 'And if a storm comes along and starts buffeting you, just hold on tight to a tree. There is no way you will be able to control the bubble so just sit it out — you'll be fine.' He glanced up at the sky, which looked calm and blue with a few puffy white clouds.

I took a deep breath. At that moment the elfin notes of a penny whistle floated down to us on the ground from a tree across the other side of the river. It was James, taking a break from rigging a tree. Jake grabbed a walkie-talkie: 'James, do you read me? I don't want to alarm you, but I thought I'd better just warn you — there's a band of morris dancers on their way.'

The radio crackled and James came through. 'Oh no! They're taking over the forest! Escape while you can,' he said. Then there was an agonized 'Help!' fading to nothing. I laughed and felt better. Right, it was time to get out of here.

I bounced off the ground, using my legs, and there was a moment of inertia before the balloon lifted me a few metres, then sank down again. We emptied out some of the water, and I started to pull on the rope, feeding it through the karabiners and travelling upwards. I tried not to look down and concentrated instead on the amazing view that was unfolding before me as I climbed higher. I even started to enjoy the sensation of floating, until I was reminded that 210 cubic metres of material acts like a ship's sail: the slightest breeze sets it dancing about and rocking the little seat. 'Steady . . . ' I said to myself, and my hands tightened on the rope.

The frame of the balloon was bristling with cameras so that I could record my experiences up in the canopy. I had to try to look cool. I went on, up and up, pulling hard on the rope that ran steeply in front of me until I was at the top of the tallest tree along the river. I brushed through its bushy crown and immediately felt better, cocooned in foliage. The bubble caught on the branches around me and I had to yank it free. I had a moment of panic when I wondered if a branch might puncture it, then remembered that Laurent had told me that the material is very tough and the balloon has a double envelope so that even if the outer layer is torn, no helium can escape.

'You're fine, you're fine,' I said to myself under my breath but I emerged from the crown of the tree and a wide gap opened up between me and the next, with a clear view to the forest floor 80 metres below. My stomach turned. It was like sitting in a swing suspended from the window-ledge on the twentieth floor of a skyscraper. As I pulled myself gingerly across the gap there was a strong gust of wind. The seat spun round, and I yo-yoed wildly up and down while I caught glimpses of the ground spinning between my feet. I was reeling with vertigo. The blustery wind made it difficult to drag the bubble along the rope and I struggled to reach the next tree where I could anchor myself. When I got to it I wrapped my arms round a branch as though it was a long-lost friend.

Now, safely wedged, I took in the view over the roof of the forest. It was hummocked, coloured with endless different greens, and stretched out as far as the eye could see. I was surrounded by the hum of insects, then heard the raucous cackle of a hornbill. Below me I caught a tiny move-ment — a squirrel — while nearer to hand a determined squadron of ants was climbing from a branch on to the rigging of my chair.

I was in another world. A third of all rainforest animals live in the canopy, spending their whole lives among its aerial walkways, never venturing to the ground. Suddenly I spotted a troop of monkeys travelling away from me. It was strange to think that life in the treetops was a part of human evolutionary history, but although I had lost what must once have been an innate head for heights I planned to spend a lot of time up here over the next few weeks, getting to know some of our closest relatives and trying to find out why the canopy is such a great place to live.

2

High Society

The forests of Sabah are one of the last strongholds of the orang-utan, but even here they are rarely seen as they lead a solitary life high in the canopy. Our first glimpse was of a mass of orange hair, thick, long, straight, and hanging from what we surmised was a forearm. Then the vegetation moved and, with a long belch, he came into view, swinging from one arm while reaching out with the other across a gap of about three metres to grab the branch of a neighbouring tree. He missed, and had to swing back and forth before he had gained enough momentum to cross the gap. The narrow branch bowed as he gripped it, reaching for another with his long opposable big toe acting like a thumb and giving him a hand-like grip. When he had a firm grasp on both new branches he let go of the first tree. They bowed under his weight, bringing him nearly to the trunk where he climbed on to a fatter limb, picked a large durian fruit and peered down at us on the ground.

The canopy has much to offer its residents but before you can reap the benefits of the high life you have to be able to get around. Orang-utans are the largest animals that live permanently in the trees and are masters of the art of treetop travel, regularly moving around at heights of around 60 metres. This makes them difficult to film in the wild so before we arrived at Danum Valley we had visited an orang-utan orphanage near Pankanlangbun, in Central Kalimantan. It had been established by Professor Birute Galdikas, the world's leading authority on orang-utan behaviour. Birute has studied orang-utans for thirty years in Tanjang Puting National Park, and is now focusing her efforts on protecting forests and rescuing the orang-utans: they are not only victims of deforestation but also of the devastating fires that have swept recently through the forests of Borneo. Over the last few decades 80 per cent of their forests have been destroyed through logging and fire, and the world population of wild orang-utans has halved, so the life of every orphan is precious.

Birute is soft-spoken, and has a strong rapport with her charges. An infant clung to her back, its long arms wrapped round her neck. When I asked her about the current situation in Kalimantan, she told me, 'It's one step forward and two steps back. It reminds me of the Red Queen in *Alice in Wonderland*, who had to keep running as fast as she could to stay in the same place.' There are 190 orphans at Birute's centre, many of their little faces look sad and careworn despite their young age but their huge dark eyes seemed filled with anticipation when their carers rounded them up from their sleeping quarters to take them out for the day into a patch of nearby forest.

We headed out into the trees surrounded by furry orange bodies, gambolling and tumbling about. As we left behind the security of the buildings some reached out to hold our hands or climbed on to their carers' backs, as they would with their mothers in the wild. About a thousand orphaned orang-utans, from several orphanages, have been returned to the wild over the last few years. It is hard to monitor them subsequently, but individuals do show up at feeding stations in times of poor fruiting, sometimes years later and with offspring of their own — showing they can survive. Providing that some forest is left for them, there is a strong chance that all the orphans we met will be returned some day to the wild. First, though, they had to learn the skills to survive there — what food to eat and how to move in the treetops.

New company is always exciting to an orang-utan, and a film crew with lots of equipment especially so. It was like being surrounded by the mob of child pickpockets in *Oliver Twist*. I was in the midst of a mêlée of about fifteen youngsters who pulled me this way and that, climbed on to my back or head and tugged insistently at the curious pouch on my belt. Soon long, dextrous fingers had opened it and their owner was examining the radio microphone inside. One rambunctious character went to investigate Si and the camera. While his back was turned, another picked up a pelican case, a hard plastic case with filming gear, and Scott rescued it in the nick of time before it went up a tree.

Mischievous orang-utans were everywhere, dashing over to play with us, then clambering up the trees. They were learning important lessons. Orang-utans aren't born climbers: while they are equipped with exceptional strength in their arms and opposable big toes that allow their feet to grip, they would usually learn how to get about from their mothers. For the first few years of their lives in the wild, they ride around on her, getting the feel of climbing and developing the ability to judge distances accurately by observing her. At three or four they start to make short forays alone through the canopy, but their mothers stay ready to catch them if they falter, or form bridges for them to clamber across when gaps are too wide. Gradually they learn which branches will take their body weight and how to use it. But these youngsters had no mothers. And as well as the complex art of high altitude locomotion a young orang-utan has to learn how to feed itself. Both their large bodies and their large intelligent brains need a plentiful supply of food. They consume four hundred different types of fruit in Bornean rainforest, as well as flowers, young leaves, sap and insects. But the rainforest canopy is like a vast city, with a variety of opening times for its shops and restaurants. Orang-utans have to develop a sophisticated mental map of where and when food is to be found, and need to travel huge distances to get to it. An adult male's range can cover as much as forty square kilometres. A challenging time lay ahead of the orphans.

Above me, an exuberant five-year-old was swinging on a branch towards a neighbouring tree. Suddenly there was a loud snap as the branch broke, then a crash as he fell a few metres into the vegetation below. Fortunately when he scrambled out, he looked more sheepish than hurt. But some falls are more serious: only few weeks earlier a similar accident had left an infant concussed for several days. Misjudging a branch high in the treetops can cost an orang-utan its life.

In Danum Valley I had a climbing lesson of my own to discover what it is about life in the canopy that makes the risks worth taking. As a child I had done a fair amount of tree-climbing and scrambling on roofs, and had shinned up some pretty tall trees, using ropes, when I made a previous television series, but all of that paled into insignificance when I was shown the trees I had to climb in Borneo. Just looking up at them my stomach did somersaults. Fortunately I was in good hands. James has been rigging and climbing trees for ten years and is as cool-headed and trustworthy as anyone I've ever met. Andy, who works with James much of the time, does a lot of tree surgery in the UK, he's ex army and as far as I can tell he isn't fazed by anything.

Between them they've probably climbed about 10,000 trees. They were also sympathetic, and didn't make me feel foolish for being scared. As James said, 'If you're not a bit nervous about climbing 150 feet up, there's something wrong with you!' I suspect that their notion of fear is nothing more than a slightly raised adrenaline level as opposed to the gut-wrenching paralysis that the rest of us might feel, but it was comforting to know that I wasn't expected to be blasé about the experience.

The air in the forest was heavy with humidity. It was early afternoon as we sweated uphill carrying several plastic red and yellow climbing bags and cases of filming equipment. Rope is heavy — 8 kilos per 100 metres James reliably informed me — and I was glad we weren't carrying the whole two kilometres we had brought with us. We were planning to climb several trees to capture images of their many residents, and fortunately James and Andy had done much of the rigging while we had been in the cinebulle and the bubble.

The forest was quiet — unlike us, most of the animals were sensibly conserving their energy at this time of day. Sun filtered down through chinks in the canopy, creating a dappled pattern on the dark forest floor. Occasionally the steady 'took, took, tu-rook' of a barbet interrupted the midday lull, and then a long series of loud, clear notes, the last few rising in pitch and tempo. It was the courtship call of a male Argus pheasant, Sabah's largest, most spectacular ground-dwelling bird. He was trying to attract females to his dancing ground, an area four or five metres across from which he had scrupulously cleared the leaves in order to display and encourage the females to mate with him.

In the muddy path there were deep hoof prints, two curved marks with little triangular impressions behind them: bearded pigs. These were the tracks we discovered most commonly, but occasionally you might come across the larger hoofprints of a Sambar deer, or even the pawprints of an Oriental small-clawed otter, a Malay civet, or marbled cat. The chance of seeing any of these animals is remote, especially in the middle of the day, but if you look closely there were plenty of others to observe. Ant trails criss-crossed the path, and a three-horned rhinoceros beetle ambled along a liana. He was impressive, nearly the size of my hand, with three enormous horns curving out of his head, each about five centimetres long. Dark brown, almost black, in the shade, he turned a glorious rich red-brown, the colour of Coca-Cola when light passes through it, as soon as he moved into a patch of sunlight.

A movement caught my eye. I stopped to look and saw a slender coppery coloured snake with fine hatching pattern, the same shade as a newly fallen leaf, of which there were many on the ground. I stood absolutely still and watched it move cautiously out onto the path. It was a blue-necked keelback — a beautiful snake about 75 centimetres long with a wide black chevron on its neck which was drawn out at its apex into a thin black line running down its back the length of its body. It moved very slowly and turned this way and that as if unsure where to go, stopping every now and again to flick out its tongue. I wondered whether it had sensed my vibrations as I had come up the path but then quick as a flash it lunged at a leaf, striking at it and locking its teeth into it. I was incredulous — what was it doing attacking a leaf?

An instant later, I realized that the leaf was in fact a horned leaf frog. It was stunningly good mimicry, its back was a perfect replica of a large dead leaf. It was quite a large and powerful frog about eight or nine centimetres, now puffed up and dragging itself and the snake across the ground. For a time the frog looked so strong that I thought it might throw off its assailant but then the snake flipped over showing its pastel pink underside, spiralling round and round in an attempt to get control. Finally the frog was turned on its back and I saw the snake's jaws locked in frog's belly below its deep red throat. My money was on the snake but I watched transfixed, as the life and death struggle went on for another fifteen minutes. At last the venom took hold and the frog lay still. It was an extraordinary cameo of life and death in the forest, and it made me realize that life isn't necessarily easy for snakes, despite their fearsome reputation.

But the most common animals on the forest floor, in low vegetation or on my trouser leg, were leeches. They sense your body heat and home in on you, searching for bare flesh. The common land leech has a painless bite, injecting into you an anaesthetic together with anti-coagulant, but the tiger, or painted, leech doesn't bother with an anaesthetic and gives quite a sharp nip. As leeches go, the latter are attractive, with rough stripes of orange, yellow, green and brown, but while I found them nice to look at I wasn't so keen on their drinking habits. At least when I was climbing trees I'd be out of their way.

When we arrived at the base of our tree I stared up it in disbelief. It was going to be a baptism of fire. It was a Mengarris — one of the emergents I had seen from the cinebulle. From its massive base it towered up 80 metres, its crown lost high above the rest of the canopy. Even its lowest branch was a giddy 50 metres up.

I've found in the past that when I'm climbing high it makes a big difference to me psychologically if I'm surrounded by thick vegetation. Those lower branches and scrub wouldn't make any difference if I were to fall, but they make me feel less exposed and vulnerable. This tree was not only big but, for filming purposes, it was fairly exposed. Climbing it would be like steeplejacking.

Andy rummaged through his pack, pulled out a dark green waterproof sheet and selected a spot. Within minutes, he had erected a shelter and slung a hammock beneath it. Rainstorms arrive suddenly in the tropics and it's good to be prepared. It was obvious that Andy's army training had also taught him to grab any opportunity to rest, but this wasn't one of them.

James and Andy had already rigged the Mengarris with a climbing rope and a safety rope, but one more climbing rope had to go up before we could start. While Scott and Si discussed how to capture my epic ascent, Andy and James worked on the final rope. 'Do you want to have a go?' Andy said turning to me as I stood gazing up at the tree. I must have looked as though I was in need of distraction.

Getting a rope up a tree of such scale is no mean feat. It is catapulted over a branch with a giant sling fixed to a wooden pole about 6 feet long. Into the sling you place a 'throw bag', a small bean bag carrying about 65 metres of thin cord. This is then attached to a thicker cord and finally a rope.

Andy handed me the sling and showed me what to do. Holding the pole upright, I jammed my foot against its base to keep it from slipping. With the other hand I reached up and pulled down steadily on the sling, locking my arm and keeping it close in to the pole until I was down on one knee with the sling impossibly taut. Then all that was required was to take aim at my chosen branch and release the sling, catapulting the throw bag and string into the air and with any luck, over the chosen branch. At least that was the theory.

My first couple of shots looped lamely into the air far from my target branch. 'I think I could probably get into that tree over there,' I said, pointing to a sapling. Andy tried to make a few encouraging noises about my efforts but it just wasn't going to happen and I handed the sling back to him. After just a few attempts Andy had the rope over the right branch.

Now it was just a matter of carefully pulling the cord and then the rope over, being careful not to snag it in the branches and then securing it to a substantial root at the base of the tree.

In the world of tree climbing there is a bewildering array of knots to get to grips with. There are bowlines and figure of eight knots, Italian hitches and for this occasion, a bunny knot with two 'ears' that could be clipped to two independent anchors, making it extra secure. I tied what I hoped was a bunny knot and showed it to James. 'Fraid not' he said shaking his head. I tried tying another and yanked it to test whether it would take any weight. It didn't give but it didn't look convincing either. 'Better knot?' I asked. I handed the end of the rope back to him. He tied the knot and showed it to me. 'Better not' he said undoing it and tying it properly before attaching it to the anchor points with a couple of slings and karabiners.

At last we were all set. James went up first, and then it was my turn. I wriggled into my harness, attached my 'rocker' to the safety rope and gave it a tug to double-check that it locked. (A rocker allows the rope to run freely through it, but locks if there is an abrupt downward pull.) Then I attached my hand ascender, or jumar, to the climbing rope, double-checked that my karabiners were done up, slipped into my foot loops, took a deep breath, and started climbing upwards. There was a lot of give in the rope, as usual, and for the first few metres I found myself bouncing around and not making much progress. 'Andy, would you grab the end for her?'

James shouted down. That helped, and gradually, as I gained height, the weight of the rope below me kept it steady and progress became easier.

It is hard work, but you are not relying on your arms to pull you up, rather you are pushing up with your legs. The jumar grips the rope by means of a metal cam that allows it to slide upwards but pinches the rope securely when weighted. The technique is to slide the jumar up the rope in front of you while your knees are bent and then push up by standing up in your foot loops. This gives you enough slack to push the jumar upwards again, and so on. You repeat this action over and over again, essentially ratcheting yourself up, and gradually you make headway up the rope.

At first I didn't really notice the height, but around 20 metres up I stopped for a break and looked around. The ground was a long way down and the bits of metal attaching me to the rope suddenly seemed no more substantial than a couple of large safety-pins. James and Andy had assured me that I could trust my life to the equipment: the rope would take a 2.7-tonne weight and the karabiners closer to 3 tonnes. 'That's a couple of Landrovers,' James had said. 'I don't think you have anything to worry about.' But at that height rational thought was tricky. I continued upwards, fixing my eyes on the beautiful cream and pink marbled bark of the tree.

The Mengarris felt incredibly solid, more like a cliff than a tree. John, our field assistant had told me that the Mengarris is sacred to the local people of the area: it is hollow and they believe that forest spirits live in the trunk. I asked the resident spirit quietly for its blessing, and kept moving. I began to feel like Jack climbing the Beanstalk, and wondered what world I might emerge into.

There was a bulge in the trunk at about thirty metres and I had to kick away with my feet to get past, and then I was beyond the first fork. A little higher the trunk became concave, giving me a sense of protection — only a few more metres to go. Finally I clambered into the second fork and James helped me hook on to a separate safety line. Breathless, exhausted and excited I stood up in the wide saddle and leant against a massive branch — I felt safe now in the arms of this giant. I could see for miles in every direction and peer into the crowns of neighbouring trees. Far below, I could hear the Argus pheasant calling.

Branches moved in a nearby tree and a Bornean gibbon swung into view. It was a soft grey-brown with a dark face framed by paler hair. Then two more appeared. Gibbons form lifelong pairs and this, no doubt, was a couple and their offspring. They scrutinized us with their large eyes, perhaps surprised to see such strange creatures in their world.

Only a few groups of mammals have evolved the skills needed to live up in the canopy. The vast majority of arboreal mammals around the world belong to just five groups: rodents, marsupials, carnivores, primates and bats. Apart from bats, all of these mammals have either firmly gripping hands and feet or sharp, hooked claws, essential for moving up and down trees. Climbing up is relatively straightforward but climbing down is harder, and the ankle joints of some animals, such as squirrels and margays, swivel to allow for head-first descent. Most other animals back down rather awkwardly, looking over their shoulders to see where they are going.

In order to travel along and between branches animals need to be able to grip with both hands and feet. The more things you can hold on with the better, so for some animals a prehensile tail acts like another hand. This is particularly useful in forests like those in South America with a well-connected canopy where animals don't have to jump from branch to branch but the musculature of prehensile tails makes them heavy. The thick tail of a howler monkey constitutes about 6% of its body weight, and extra weight is not something you want in the canopy.

Many tree-dwelling animals are small, below 15 kilos, and at around 90 kilos male orang-utans are at about the upper limit: any heavier, and they would be confined to the few branches that could take their weight.

When branches are too narrow for apes to walk on, they swing underneath instead, so the bigger the animal, the stronger its grip has to be. The gibbons' elongated fingers looked delicate, but they swung easily from one hand to the other through the canopy. This form of locomotion, brachiating, is an efficient way of getting through the treetops — gibbons are the fastest flightless animals in the canopy, moving at speeds of up to

35 kilometres per hour. Their long, strong arms, light bodyweight and ball-and-socket wrists make them extremely efficient, as does the pendular motion whereby the momentum of the swing provides most of the energy. Amazingly, the faster they move the less energy they expend.

As we watched, one of the gibbons danced along a branch standing upright with his arms stretched out like a tightrope walker. When moving along the top of branches, gibbons regularly walk upright rather than on all fours because their habit of hanging vertically has led to a change in hip position, giving them a more upright stance. It is now thought that our ancestors were essentially bipedal even before they came to the ground.

Because of the difficulties involved in moving through trees, most arboreal animals do not travel long distances in comparison with those that live on the ground. Even the most active canopy dwellers, like gibbons travel less than two kilometres a day, and while they can move fast, speed is not of the essence because their food consists of fruit, leaves, sap, pollen and insects. High-speed chases in pursuit of prey are tricky in the latticework of the canopy so many carnivores that live up there tend not to feed exclusively on vertebrates. Those with the greatest appetite for meat — linsangs, martens and margays — hunt mostly on the ground.

We caught a fleeting glimpse of a flying squirrel sailing across a gap below us, looking a bit like a flying frying pan, the skin stretched between its fingers and toes, its tail streaming out behind it. Borneo has more gliding mammals and reptiles than anywhere else on Earth: they have evolved in that way because of the types of trees that surround them.

One tree family dominates the lowland forests of Borneo: the Dipterocarps, whose name comes from the Greek and means 'two-winged fruit', and refers to the mature fruit's wing-like appendages. African and South American rain-forests have a fairly closed canopy structure, formed by densely packed trees of uniform height, but Dipterocarp forests are characterised by large numbers of emergents whose crowns are separated from others by as much as 10 metres. Unless they can glide most animals cannot cross such big gaps.

'Look at this.' James was pointing to a small lizard sitting near us. It was about 10 centimetres long, greyish in colour, with flecks of green and yellow, and long, slender feet. I picked it up gently, between my thumb and forefinger, just behind its head. When I opened my hand it rested calmly in my palm. I could see its eyes searching around as if it was getting its bearings. Then it jumped. We were about 40 metres up, but this was no suicide leap: little flaps opened on its neck and membranes spread out wide, like wings, supported by modified ribs. Like a skydiver it sailed through the air, gliding expertly down to a lower branch. We had just seen *Drago volans*, a flying dragon, in action. This extraordinary creature is reminiscent of the Icarosaurus, one of the first airborne vertebrates of the Triassic period, between 250–206 million years ago, and this useful trick helps it escape from danger.

Later, a kite swept over us. Powered flight is the ultimate means of travel, and birds are the deadliest killers on high, and in rainforests around the world, the canopy is a hunting ground for many different raptors. Hawks, with their short broad wings, are masters of speed and agility when flying through a dense network of branches, kites patrol the canopy by day, and owls swoop down from the trees by night. The most powerful of the aerial predators, though, are eagles. Harpy eagles are the largest in the world, with a wingspan of two metres; they dominate the canopy in Central and South America from southern Mexico to Argentina, plucking young monkeys, sloths and iguanas out of the trees with their fearsome talons. In Africa I have seen the dark shadows of a crowned eagle sweep over the trees causing pandemonium along a group of colobus monkeys — they fled, issuing high-pitched alarm chirps. In parts of South East Asia, the monkey-eating eagle, a ferocious-looking bird that is almost as powerful as the harpy eagle, eats macaques, while the crested-serpent eagle terrorises the reptile population.

The structure of the canopy at different levels determines what animals live there. Up high, the inhabitants are either restricted to a single tree or must glide or fly between them; also, they are exposed to the full force of the sun by day and the cold at night when the temperature can drop sharply. Near the ground there is very little light

and the plants are lightly constructed, supporting only small birds and animals. Most animals
live in the middle section of the canopy where
branches are thicker and lianas act as highways
between the trees. At this level the irregular
mosaic of crowns overhead means that the light
is variable encouraging a wide diversity of trees
and plentiful food — fruits, leaves, seeds and
nectar.

Although my legs felt like jelly, I felt
triumphant when I arrived back down on the
ground from the top of the Mengarris — it had
opened my eyes to a different world. In the
weeks to come I was to climb quite a few trees
and the time I spent in the canopy impressed
upon me what an extremely varied environment
it is. Not only is there a multitude of different
species of tree but every single tree is unique,
like a city where no two buildings or their
residents are the same.

In South East Asia, Dipterocarps are prime
residences. They contain up to 40 per cent of all
arboreal dwellers' nests, and monitor lizards,
flying squirrels, bees, wasps, king cobras and
hornbills all vie for the best places. There are
eight species of hornbill in Sabah and the pairs
search out suitable homes together. Like many
others they don't excavate their own nest holes
but rely on finding somewhere empty and quite
spacious. Competition for nest holes is often
fierce as they are in short supply. Sometimes a
hole is created when a branch falls off, but a
cavity might begin its life as the result of a
woodpecker's drilling. Then it is enlarged into a

hole by a fungus, which attracts a colony of bees, and then perhaps a bear, whose claws widen it in the search for honey.

You often hear the fantastic sound of the great hornbill, flying overhead in the forest; its five-foot wing span produces a rush of air at each powerful downward stroke. Many species of hornbill are now endangered, and scientists are keen to find out as much as possible about their breeding behaviour. A pair of binoculars is enough to see a lot of what goes on outside their nests and the males can sometimes be seen delivering food. However, tiny 'lipstick' cameras installed in a hornbill nest hole can provide a close look into their private lives. First, the female great hornbill lines the nest with material brought to her by the male. Once it is ready she seals herself in, closing the entrance with mud, sticky foodstuffs and droppings, leaving just a narrow slit through which the male can feed her and the chicks. She remains there for months, while her partner provides her with fruit, beetles, snakes, geckos, scorpions, bats and even the young of other birds. Only when she is satisfied that he can provide for her does she commit herself to breeding. She lays just one egg and incubates it for up to 42 days. We watched footage of a female who had nested in the same hole for ten years. Her chick had just hatched and she sat for long periods with her eye to the slit, watching the world outside — not out of boredom but because she was keeping guard over the nest. Any animal appearing suddenly at the entrance is attacked with her bill, while she gives loud alarm calls. She also keeps the nest scrupulously clean, backing up to the slit when she defecates, and throwing out her chicks' droppings when it tries to do likewise and misses.

The canopy is not only full of penthouse suites, it also boasts amazing rooftop 'gardens'. Perched 50 metres high, they are filled with the drooping, antler-like fronds of the staghorn fern, little red flowers like snap-dragons and exquisite orchids, such as the delicate white swan's necklace, the long dishevelled locks of the Medusa, or the sweetly scented elephant's ear. In tropical rainforests where most of the light at lower levels is blocked out by big trees, epiphytes, plants that live on trees, have easy access to sunlight. On some trees the epiphytes are so abundant that their leaf area may exceed that of the tree.

On our last day in Danum, we visited a particularly magnificent garden at the top of a tall Dipterocarp. When I looked up into the tree it appeared that a flock of giant birds had nested in the branches. In fact, it was half a dozen bird's nest ferns, the largest of all epiphytes. It was not until I was up in the tree directly alongside one that I could appreciate how large they really are, some measured nearly two metres across. It seemed an extraordinary thing to find up there — a vast mass of strap-like fronds that emerged from a gigantic clump of decaying vegetation as though a digger had excavated a huge clump of earth sprouting a prize-winning cabbage and balanced it precariously on a branch.

Like other epiphytes, bird's nest ferns are not parasitic: they do not live at the tree's expense, but simply colonise a space on a branch in the sunshine, growing slowly by picking up traces of minerals in rainwater and trapping soil and dust particles to build up an 'epiphyte mat' along the branch. Some epiphytes send out a net of aerial roots to trap debris, while the leaves of others, such as the litter basket epiphyte of Central America, *Anthurium salviniae*, grow to form a rosette that funnels valuable detritus and rain to the centre of the plant. Bird's nest ferns make themselves a nest of their own rotting leaves, which acts as a source of nourishment for new leaves. The weight of these plants is considerable: I estimated that the one I was sitting next to probably weighed close to 200 kilos, about the same as a baby elephant.

The combined weight of several epiphytes can sometimes run to several tonnes, which may eventually prove too much for a tree. The loss of a branch is a high price for a tree to pay and it seems that some species may have developed strategies to rid themselves of their hangers-on: in the Amazon, trees such as Terminalia periodically slough off great sheets of bark, dislodging any epiphytes, to reveal the pale pink bark beneath that has given them their nickname, 'tourist trees'; other trees have developed smooth bark, which sheds water rapidly and prevents the build-up of algae or other substances that epiphyte seeds need to germinate. The best defence system that I have come across, however, is used by a tree called

Leptospermum flavescens, a species belonging to the tea tree family. The tree has cavities in its base where a species of Crematogaster ants live. They excavate a series of tunnels that emerge high in the crown where they scour the branches, removing all epiphytes, moss and lichens.

There is a fascinating twist in the relationship between epiphytes and trees. It has long been known that trees are recompensed to some extent by epiphytes, which collect moisture from the air that is slowly released during dry periods. Now, though, it has been discovered that the trees may benefit more directly from their gardens. Recently, Nalini Nadkarni, a canopy scientist with the Smithsonian Tropical Research Institute in Panama, found that many host trees grow aerial root systems identical to those below ground but these emerge from high branches and obtain minerals and water by growing directly into the tangled mats of rotting vegetation formed by the epiphytes.

I prodded under my bird's nest fern to see if I could find any aerial tree roots. They weren't evident, but a little brown skink hurried out from between the fronds and disappeared. This, I realised, was another way in which epiphytes pay their rent: they provide homes to a great many animals, whose waste, and other organic material from the canopy, fertilises the ground at its base. In one bird's nest fern alone you might find 300,000 individual animals: termites, ants, beetles, worms, centipedes, geckos, snakes and spiders — a veritable Noah's Ark of creatures. Of all the different animals found living on a rainforest tree nearly three-quarters make their home somewhere in one of these hanging gardens.

As if to underline this fact, the branch around me was now covered with giant forest ants, the largest ants in the world. Ants have different 'castes' with different jobs. Among giant forest ants the soldiers have mandibles that are savage: I put out my hand to block one, which sank them into my hand. Fortunately I was wearing a tough glove, but the mandibles locked so firmly into the fabric that their owner was unable to let go.

Ants not only have close associations with trees — many species are closely involved with the epiphytes they live in. Shrubby baboon's head ants use the epiphyte *Myrmecodia tuberosa* for their homes, de-luxe multi-roomed apartments with an organic touch. The root base of this plant is structured inside like a honeycomb, which provides living space for the ants. Some roots are used for living and reproduction, while others store the ants' waste. This in turn makes useful fertilizer for the epiphyte, which grows extra roots into these storage areas to tap the nutrients inside. So the plants benefit by obtaining nutrients and protection whilst the ants get prime real estate in the canopy.

Giant forest ants have underground nests but forage in huge 3D territories in the canopy, using bird's nest ferns as base camps. They partition the fern's detritus bole, chewing out living chambers, and use it as a hub for their daily foraging. At the end of the day, they return to the nest on the forest floor.

By late afternoon the sky was darkening to the north and it would soon be time for us to return to the forest floor. However, we hadn't quite finished filming the ferns and their occupants. 'We should be okay for a bit,' James said, assessing the ominous clouds that were piling up on the horizon. Ten minutes later, we felt the wind picking up in the trees around us, and in the distance thunder rolled. 'I guess we've got about another five minutes and then we're going to have to bail out — fast.' James was frowning now as we rushed to transfer from our fixed point lines in the tree to our climbing ropes. Then, all of a sudden, we heard the roar of the wind like a diesel train approaching at full speed.

The arrival of a tropical storm is exciting to watch on the ground, but when you're perched on a little branch at the top of a tall tree it's something else. James radioed down to Andy and asked him to stand by. I unclipped the karabiner from my anchor point and swung off my perch. By now the tree crowns were swaying wildly, moving back and forth by several metres, and the first spots of rain were falling. I was at the bottom within minutes, and unhooked myself quickly to free the ropes for the others. As the heavens opened around us down came the camera protected in a plastic kit bag, followed remarkably swiftly by Si, his descender steaming with the heat of friction against the rope. He unclipped it from his rope and chucked it to me 'There you go'. 'I'm not going to fall for that one again!' I said. Last time he'd thrown his descender to me I had caught it automatically only to find it scorched my hand. Minutes later James arrived on the ground, he was soaking wet. Safely back down on the ground we huddled under the protection of Andy's shelter while the storm raged around us.

Later, over a beer, we reviewed the footage from the cameras we had rigged in another tree and saw the storm's full fury. It must have been hair-raising for the animals up there: the crowns were swaying back and forth by four or five metres, twisting and turning, which must have exerted extraordinary tension on the trunks and roots. The rain hammered down on the leaves. This too can be overwhelming for the trees. They shut down the breathing pores in their leaves and their crowns act like umbrellas, sheltering the trunks and protecting the soil around the roots. Rain also creates ideal conditions for fungi: any water remaining on the leaves encourages its growth. In temperate forests leaves come in many different shapes, but in tropical rainforests they are more standardised in an oval with an elongated tip — a 'drip tip': it acts as a spout and channels water away. Essential maintenance in protecting the canopy.

The storm made a dramatic finale to our stay in Danum. The next day we were off to Thailand.

3

Curious Liaisons

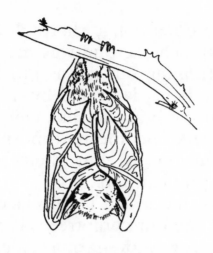

A tiny sunbird was drinking nectar, oblivious to my presence just a few feet away. Its iridescent feathers caught the morning light, shimmering deep purplish blue, while its long curved bill probed deep into a red flower shaped like a flaming rocket-head. Behind it, in electric blue and glossy black, a fairy bluebird also busied itself among the flowers. We were sitting high in the branches of a tall, slim coral tree and from every direction birds were flying in: a banquet was taking place, a kaleidoscope of colour among the crimson blooms. A couple of vibrant green hanging parrots arrived, followed by a little spiderhunter, another parrot and then, a few minutes later, a black-headed bulbul joined us, dressed in brilliant yellow with a smart black crest. In our grubby khaki clothes Si, James and I were poorly turned out in comparison with the birds and we sat among them like oversized gate-crashers. They didn't seem to mind, though; they flitted from flower to flower and came and went from the tree with only one concern — to feast.

'Ouch!' Another long, sharp thorn had dug into my thigh. The setting was magnificent and the guests stunning but it was proving tricky to film: we were being lacerated by the thorns that bristled from the branches like nails sticking out of an old plank and the mid-morning sun was beating down on us, but there was a more intransigent problem too.

These days, fewer and fewer places are off the beaten track and our coral tree was not in one of them. A nearby wide tarmac road carried a constant stream of traffic and the forest sounds were drowned by engines straining up the hill, the whine of mopeds and the tooting of horns. We were in Khao Yai National Park in Thailand, a rich, beautiful forest covering an area of 2168 square kilometres in the uplands north of Bangkok. Khao Yai attracts over a million visitors a year and its popularity is encouraging: it reflects a growing appreciation for the local wildlife and brings in revenue that will ensure the park's future. But it can make filming a frustrating business.

I shifted awkwardly on my branch, trying to get the circulation back into my leg. We had been waiting for half an hour for the traffic noise to subside. However, it was approaching lunchtime and the sounds from the road were dying away. Eventually there was quiet, except for the hum of insects and the breeze among the leaves. From the base of the tree Jake called, 'Okay, sound is good,' and Si turned on the camera.

'Running up . . . Speed,' he said and nodded to me. I turned towards him and caught the seat of my trousers on one of the tree's vicious spikes. But this was no time for self-consciousness: if we were to get the sequence finished that day I had to grab the moment. I was here to talk about flowers.

The flowering of any tree is an important occasion. In most rainforests around the world one species or another will be flowering at any given time throughout the year, but in some parts of Southeast Asia this is not the case. Instead, there is a curious phenomenon called 'masting' when a variety of different species all blossom together. Every six to ten years there is a major masting event — a massive synchronised flowering which can cover an area of 100 square kilometres. Individual trees often flower in close succession, so that as the blooms of one tree fade another opens its flowers, filling the forest with heavy scent for three to four months.

They are hard to predict and recent evidence suggests that they may be triggered by the arrival of something called the El Niño Southern Oscillation, a periodic shift in tropical Pacific weather patterns. Unfortunately we had just missed a masting event in Danum valley and so instead found ourselves up the coral tree in Thailand. Though less spectacular the coral tree is a reliable annual source of food . . . and it brings to it a varied clientele from far and wide. But the provision of nectar to fairy bluebirds and hanging parrots is not simple generosity on the part of the coral tree. It is payment for an important service. In order to reproduce, plants must be pollinated by the transfer of the pollen grains that contain male sex cells to the female stigma of the flower. The coral tree, like 90 per cent of flowering plants, depends on animals to make the vital delivery. The origins of this arrangement date back millions of years. Animals became interested in pollen long before plants started to use them as couriers: early beetles and flies, among other insects, used their grinding mandibles to destroy the cones of Jurassic plants to get at it. However, by the end of the age of the dinosaurs, a new group of plants, the Angiosperms, had started to attract insects with rich nectar, bright colours and alluring perfumes to enlist them as pollen distributors. They had turned the previous insect-plant relationship on its head.

Flowering plants now employ a wide range of animals to perform this service. I watched a parrot probe a coral flower, picking up sticky pollen on its beak. When it visited another blossom, it would transfer the pollen to a strategically placed stigma. Strewn below us on the forest floor was a carpet of red petals from the blooms that had opened and died within a matter of days. In that short time they had fulfilled their purpose: they had been fertilised to produce the seeds of a new generation.

Like many rainforest species, coral trees grow far apart from each other, which means they must attract pollinators that travel long distances. To lure birds from their flight over the forest, canopy trees put on extravagant, eye-catching displays of red, purple, yellow, white or orange — flamboyant beacons scattered about the green of the canopy — to capture the attention of their target audience. The coral tree's display is one of the most spectacular — there can be as many as 650,000 brilliant red flowers on one tree, producing gallons of nectar every day.

Red often appeals to birds — and bees. The latter cannot see the colour itself, but instead markings on the petals show up in their ultraviolet vision. Honeybee scouts find patches of suitable flowers, then recruit huge numbers of their clan to feed on them. This efficient strategy enables them to monopolise much of the available nectar in African and Asian rainforests and may explain why in these forests there are fewer bee species than there are in South American rainforests. There, a variety of different bees fills the same niche, but the introduction of honeybees may have a huge impact on this.

In Africa, several years ago, I was chased by bees, and was now keeping alert for an ominous droning — the last thing I wanted was to discover I was sitting on their dinner table, especially when it was 35 metres up in the air and the only exit was a tree-trunk covered with thorns.

I looked down at our 'base camp' at the foot of

51

the tree where Scott and Jake were lounging around comfortably on a rain poncho spread out like a picnic blanket. Andy was snoozing in his hammock. 'I think we've finished up here' I said to Scott on the walkie-talkie 'Can we come down now . . . please.'

We climbed back down the trunk, collecting scratches and grazes along the way, and had lunch in the cool shade below. Not all the forest flowers bloom in the canopy, and year round in the dark underbelly of the forest there is a ceaseless procession of beetles, wasps, moths, orchid bees and butterflies looking for a meal. The plants that need to attract them sprout small, scented flowers from their lower branches or trunks.

If a tree can ensure that its pollinator goes from it only to another of its kind, there is less pollen wastage, so some have developed methods of enticing one species in particular — perhaps by placing the nectar so that only the target can get at it. Sometimes several trees of the same family depend on one species of pollinator, in which case they take it in turns to flower over a few weeks so that they don't compete for the same services. This prevents the pollinators starving, because if they did all of the trees would suffer.

Where masting occurs, the relationship between tree and pollinator may involve a third party that sustains the pollinator during the times when the tree is not in bloom. Some dipterocarps such as Shorea are pollinated by tiny insects called thrips whose 'boom and bust' population cycles can be linked to periods of masting. The thrips breed in the flowers well before they open so that they mature within the buds. The flowers open at dusk and the thrips spend the night feasting on the pollen. At noon the next day all the flowers fall off the plant, each propeller-shaped rosette carrying its own batch of pollen covered thrips. These trees are emergents — so carried on the wind, a million miniature thrip arks can cover some distance. If they land under another Shorea, the thrips disembark and fly up into the budding flowers, to begin the process again.

One tree family and their pollinators have developed such a close relationship that neither can survive without the other. There are 900 species of fig, and each relies on its own species of Agaonid wasp to pollinate it. Fig flowers do not open: instead, hundreds of tiny brown flowers lie crammed together, concealed inside a tightly closed fruit. Inside it, a strange and wonderful drama is played out. A female wasp pushes herself through a snug gap in the fleshy inner rind of the unripe fig, often losing her wings or part of an antenna in the process. Throughout her life she carries pollen tucked into tiny recessed pockets on the thorax. Her purpose in the fig is to lay eggs, but as her long ovipositor probes deep within the flower, she transfers the pollen to the female flowers, fertilising them. Then she dies, leaving her larvae to feed off the ripening seeds in their flower cradles. Many seeds are destroyed, but for the fig it's a price worth paying.

As the wasp larvae develop, they prevent the fruit developing so that it isn't eaten by passing monkeys or birds. After a month, wingless males emerge, fertilise the females still trapped inside the fruit and then tunnel out. As air floods in, it triggers the production of hundreds of tiny male flowers laden with pollen. The females gather it into their thorax pockets and leave by the males' exit holes. They must now seek fresh blossoms inside another unripe fig of the same species, just as their mothers did, so the coffin of one generation becomes the womb of the next — and another host fig is fertilised too.

Insects are responsible for pollinating an estimated 90 per cent of plants in South East Asia. But there is a downside: hungry larvae can consume tonnes of leaf matter every year at considerable loss to the trees. Fortunately, forests have an effective pest-control system.

A steep rocky path led us up to a sheer cliff, with caves carved into it: its name, Khao Luk Chang means 'young elephant' in Thai, and if you approach from a certain angle you can sometimes detect the shape in the rock face at the entrance. We passed through a couple of small caves, then came to a considerably larger one — from which came the choking smell of uric acid.

We waited in the shadows while the sun set over the forested hills. Many animals were tucking themselves away for the night, but others were waking up, ready for the night shift. The forest population was about to explode . . .

At 6.03 p.m., we heard a murmur within the cave. The sound built rapidly until it became a loud, incessant rustling like a brisk wind blowing through dry leaves. A small shape darted out of the cave. Its fanned wings were silhouetted for an instant against the pink sky, and then it was gone. It was followed by another, and another. Within moments the sky around us was a blur of movement as thousands of wrinkle-lipped bats emerged from the cave. Over half a million live crowded together in these caves and at dusk they leave *en masse*, some sixty thousand pouring out every minute.

The orange orb of the sun emerged from behind a low-lying cloud, and the bats' wings glowed deep red as they swept past me. I could feel a breeze on my face created by their wing-beats — the sound was intense and the flickering motion made me dizzy. And that is the point: this vast synchronised flight is part of the bats' survival strategy. Peregrine falcons and bat hawks perch on cliff edges, ready to dive when an opportunity presents itself, but they are unable to pick out a target in the swirling mêlée. Any bats that stray from the main stream are swiftly taken out, but as long as they stay with the rest they are safe.

Wrinkle-lipped bats are insect-eaters and every night they pour into the forest to hunt. There are about a thousand species of bat worldwide (110 in Thailand alone), making up a quarter of all known species of mammal. Of these, some 70 per cent are insect-eaters and the role they play in pest control cannot be overestimated. In a single night in Thailand the bats of Khao Luk Chang can consume more than five thousand kilos of insects. By controlling the numbers of leaf-eating insects, they restrict the damage to the trees they feed on, so helping to maintain the balance of the canopy ecosystem.

It is not just bats that come to life at night. The forest is like a city that never sleeps, and the road is one of the best places to see wildlife after dark. As we travelled from the bat cave back to our bungalows, eyes shone in the headlights, and we saw the sleek shape of a yellow-throated marten disappearing into the grass, or the round, ambling figure of a Malayan porcupine, its long black and white quills spraying out from its back and short spiky ones sticking up from its head.

Just a few kilometres from home we rounded a corner to find a queue of cars reversing towards us. A young bull elephant was wandering along the middle of the road, stopping every few yards to pull at some leaves and pop them into his mouth. We backed up our minibuses to where the road widened, and got out. Jeb and Pe'ak, our drivers, took control and started to direct the traffic. We stood and watched the elephant for a while, while it calmly went on with its meal. Eventually, Jeb encouraged us back into the minibus, and drove round it.

To experience more of the forest nightlife, and in particular that of the canopy, I was scheduled to sleep in the treetops for a few nights. Khao Yai is largely primary forest with relatively little understorey vegetation. As we walked through it carrying the equipment and supplies we would

56

need for the sleepover, I caught glimpses of a group of pig-tailed macaques rustling through the thick carpet of dry leaves, the youngsters falling about playfully while adult males, almost twice the size of the females, swaggered past. Here and there a shaft of late-afternoon light illuminated the slatted fronds of a tropical palm or picked out the detail in a patch of mottled bark.

We stopped on a slope at the base of a stout tree. James and Andy had rigged it with ropes, a small wooden platform three-quarters of the way up, supported by metal struts lashed to the trunk with heavy-duty slings. James and Andy had spent two days rigging the tree and setting up the platform before we arrived; then it took another whole day to set up infrared lights and remote infrared cameras under Si's direction.

In order to sleep and film up the tree for several nights we were going to need more than our toothbrushes. All in all we had one and a half kilometres of rope, which gave us three access ropes and three more for moving around in the canopy; two 100-watt and two 150-watt lights, 20 metres of cable and five car batteries. In addition we had a computer, two camera monitors, a couple of Tilly lamps, sleeping-bags, hammocks, torches, bananas, chocolate, water and a thermos of '3 in 1', which was one of Pe'ak's specialities: shockingly sweet, strong coffee guaranteed to keep you totally wired all night. We had decided to leave the first-aid kit on the ground. Last time it had been brought up and left overnight in the tree, a rat had chewed through the layers of canvas and cardboard, then eaten several packets of pills, including one of Imodium, a powerful anti-laxative, which it must have seriously regretted.

Dusk fell, and the shrill whine of cicadas intensified around us. James climbed the tree first, then hoisted up the camera and sound gear with a pulley. When it was all up top, the rest of us followed. I waited my turn on the ropes, then shouldered my pack, which held a few things for the night, including a notebook, pens, camera, spare torch and, most important, my 'pee bags'. I'd got them from a souvenir shop and they seemed ideal for a girl caught short in the canopy, although I suspected they weren't going to do much for my dignity. At least it was dark, and perhaps we could switch off the infrared lights so I wouldn't be lit up in a rosy glow.

I flicked my head torch on, attached my rocker to a safety rope, clipped my hand ascender onto my climbing rope, slipped the rope through the croll at my waist and started to climb. I knew the drill well by now and no longer felt obliged to triple-check everything, but this was the first time I'd climbed in the dark. Immediately the ground melted into blackness, broken only by a stray torch beam. At night the forest recedes and your world shrinks to the little pool of light made by your head-torch. Climbing trees in daylight, I had been very aware of the space around and especially below me, but now I examined the nooks and crannies in the trunk, a small white moth that landed on the edge of my pool of light, and the leaves my shoulders brushed on the way up.

The platform was around 3 × 1.5 metres, which sounds quite large until you put five people and mountains of gear on it. Si, Jake, James and Andy were already up there, checking that the equipment was working and properly tethered to the tree. They planned to film me arriving at the top, so I waited on the rope, switched off my torch and hung suspended in the dark, breathing in the heady fragrance of some invisible night flower and listening to the chorus of frogs far below.

At night the character of the forest changes completely. Different animals are awake, whose senses, unlike ours, are attuned to the dark: martens, with their keen sense of smell, or lorises, with enormous round eyes and acute night vision. On the forest floor hunters are on the prowl. Earlier, Toh, a local wildlife artist who was also acting as our filming assistant, had pointed out a fur-ball in the undergrowth that looked much like that of a domestic cat, but was tennis-ball sized and had been left there by a tiger. When you are perched in a tree overnight in this part of the world, the conversation turns naturally to tigers and, specifically, how high they can climb. In fact, they would have been hard pushed to reach our platform, but the park is also home to black and clouded leopards, to whom the climb would have presented no problem. Nevertheless it was likely that they were more frightened of us then we were of them, and would stay well clear. At least, we hoped so.

If we were quiet we might glimpse a slow loris or a civet on one of the infrared cameras. I was especially hoping to spot a binturong, or bearcat, one of the canopy's most curious nocturnal creatures. Binturongs are related to civets and genets but they are more heavy-set and don't really look like they belong way up in the branches of trees. A little under a metre in length, it has a wide, open face with a shortish muzzle, round ears edged with white, crescent-shaped markings and long hair tufts, shaggy black fur and a thick prehensile tail as long as its body. It moves slowly in the trees, using its tail for balance or to cling to branches while it feeds on ripe fruit, especially figs. Although our tree was a fig, no binturongs arrived that particular night.

We filmed into the small hours, then Si and Jake headed for the ground, leaving me to unroll my sleeping-bag on the platform and keep an eye on the remote camera monitor. I was also armed with a mini digital video camera to capture anything exciting that happened. James and Andy had slung their hammocks above me, to be on hand in case of emergency, but for now I was alone, perched on a couple of planks 30 metres up a tree in the middle of the jungle night.

I sat and watched the darkness, glancing periodically at the monitor, which was feeding me an image of a large branch on the other side of the tree. Eventually I lay down in my sleeping-bag. I was exhausted, but too excited to sleep, listening to the hooting of an owl across the valley and the soft, high-pitched wolf-whistle of a nightjar. Above, I could just trace the outline of the branches and see a few stars twinkling through the leaves. To the southeast the ground sloped away steeply, giving me a window to the sky and a clear view of the Southern Cross shining brilliantly over the dark shapes of trees.

Closer to me, the flickering light of fireflies wove through the branches. By now it must have been four or five a.m. and I felt surprisingly cold. Metal jangled round my waist as I reached into my pack for a jumper: I was tethered to the tree by my harness with two safety ropes — James had made sure I wasn't going anywhere in the night. I dived into my jumper and snuggled deep into my sleeping-bag, or as far down as I could without my 'umbilical cords' jamming the zip. Then peering into the dark void over the edge of the platform I was reminded that I was sleeping on a tiny veranda 30 metres up in the air and the tug of the ropes round me was happily reassuring.

Overhead, leaves rustled and I peered up into the branches, but even though my eyes had become more accustomed to the darkness I couldn't see anything. Also, whatever it was, it was in the wrong place to be picked up by the remote cameras. I turned on my torch. Twin saucers of light glowed at me from the dark foliage. The animal moved along the branch, and a long tail with eye-catching stripes came into view. I caught my breath. It was a banded linsang, an elegant cat-like animal, padding expertly along an aerial walkway over my bed. Not much is known about this secretive animal except that it feeds at night on lizards, small rodents and birds.

The rest of the first night passed fairly uneventfully in the canopy and I slept fitfully occasionally waking at the jangle of karabiners at my waist and with the whispering of leaves or the snapping of a twig woven into my dreams. I was surprised by the absence of bats. Where were all those wrinkle-lipped creatures I had watched surging into the forest from the cave?

On our second night I got out the bat detector. Bats use 'echolocation' to navigate through the branches and find their insect prey; they emit high-pitched squeaks and listen to the echoes to build a picture of their immediate environment. The sounds are mostly too high for the human ear to pick up, but the bat detector slows them down to make them deeper so that we can hear them. Different species of bat have different calls.

There are two ways to use a bat detector: you can find out whether a particular species is around by turning the detector to pick up its unique frequency, or you can simply check what is out there by setting it to pick up a broad range of different frequencies. Wrinkle-lipped bats utter calls from 23 to 40 kilohertz with maximum energy (that is, the strongest signal) concentrated at around 25 kilohertz. I set the detector accordingly and used it to scan the vegetation. Nothing. But wrinkle-lipped bats catch insects above the canopy, so perhaps they were out of range. Then I tried searching for a range of frequencies, and the result was instantaneous — the acoustic equivalent of night-vision goggles. Suddenly the air was full of strange rumblings and high-pitched peeps that I had not heard before. Not all of the sounds were made by bats, but after a while I picked up calls between 40 and 45 kilohertz, with a maximum energy of 42 kilohertz that lasted 10 milliseconds.

Bat calls can be recorded and identified by a computer program called BatsoundPro, which searches for a match in its database or allows various aspects of the calls to be measured and analysed. I wanted to see if I could find a match for the call I had picked up and opened the sleek black computer we had borrowed from the BBC stores in Bristol. It looked incongruous sitting on the battered tin trunk balanced on the platform that acted as my desk. I switched it on and its screen leapt into life, a bright square of incandescent blue in the dark canopy.

'We'll have to turn the brightness down,' Si said. He wanted a shot of the sonograms of the bat calls, but the contrast between the glowing screen and the surrounding darkness was too great for the DigiBeta camera. I looked for a dial on the side, back or front of the computer to no avail, then tried various screen-setting menus with an equal lack of success. Everyone had a go, but without a manual for the computer, we were stuck.

Then I heard Si say, 'Hi, is that the BBC in Bristol? Can you put me through to IT?' He was talking into his mobile. 'Hi, Tom, I'm in Thailand up a tree in the middle of the night trying to get a shot of a computer screen and I need to know how to turn down the screen brightness.' He grinned at us in the lamplight. 'He's put me on hold and they're playing 'Greensleeves'.' Eventually Tom was back on the line, suggesting we try one of the function keys. It didn't work either, but the incident was sufficiently surreal to have made it worthwhile.

In my tree 'office' I had mug-shots of some of the bats found in these parts. The bat I had heard in the canopy was probably an evening bat of the genus *Myotis*. I wasn't sure which species it was, but I had pictures of other members of its extended family, the *Vespertilionidae* — a curious-looking bunch with small eyes, large ears, with a fleshy outgrowth called a tragus, and swollen, pig-like noses. Some of the other insectivorous bats were even less attractive, with bizarre flaps called lappets on their faces and leaf-like growths that splayed out around their snouts, thought to focus the calls they emit through their noses. All of those characteristics have doubtless evolved to act as perfect transmitters and receivers in detecting the echoes of their calls as they bounce off insects in flight, allowing the bats to pinpoint their minute prey in the pitch dark.

It is not only insectivorous bats that play a crucial role in forest ecology: nectar- and fruit-eating species occur worldwide and help to maintain the diversity and regeneration of forests. Later we picked up the calls of a dawn bat, which flies between flowering trees to feed on their nectar. It is responsible for pollinating more than thirty species, including the 'king of fruits', the durian, famous for its foul smell and delicious taste. It is an important food source for both animals and local people and provides a harvest worth an estimated $120 million annually in South East Asia.

Bats are often ignored and even disliked by people all over the world — almost half of all bat species are threatened with extinction due to habitat loss and conflict with humans — yet their role in maintaining the health and diversity of forests, as well as commercial crops, cannot be overestimated. They are more effective in long-distance pollination than either insects or birds, as they travel further, sometimes covering up to 70 kilometres in a night. Around 5 per cent of all trees in South East Asia and about 14 per cent of those in New World forests rely on bats. Among the trees pollinated by dawn bats is the Petai, an important colonising species, assisting in the recovery of damaged forests. Elsewhere, bats pollinate mangoes, cottonsilk trees, cashews and dates. While cultivated bananas do not need to be pollinated to produce fruit, wild bananas, which are an essential genetic reservoir for improving cultivated varieties and combating disease, rely exclusively on bats.

A Duabanga tree, with hundreds of large white flowers clustered on the underside of its sturdy branches, stood not far from where we were and wafts of its rich fragrance floated to me on the night air. The strong scent and white or pale yellow flowers, which are conspicuous at night, are typical of trees that rely on bats to pollinate them. The flowers are strong enough to support the animals when they land on them, and they bloom at the ends of bare branches or the trunk (a phenomenon known as cauliflory) so that they are easily accessible.

The relationship between dawn bats and the Duabanga is so close that the trees, which flower on just one night of the year, produce huge quantities of nectar starting at about 7.30 p.m. to coincide with when the bats emerge hungry from their caves. I had a picture of a dawn bat among my collection and, unlike the insectivores, fruit- and nectar-eating bats have a certain charm: large eyes enable them to see the canopy at night, a dog-like muzzle helps them pick up alluring fragrances, and a long tongue allows them to probe deep into the flowers. In the picture, the dawn bat's nose was smudged with pollen, which it would deliver to the next Duabanga tree it visited.

On my last night in the canopy, I woke early as usual and lay shivering in my sleeping-bag, watching the light creep into the sky. The flat grey expanse was gradually suffused with pastel pinks and then, at last, the fiery rim of the sun appeared over a bank of low cloud, bringing a soft, warm glow to the waking forest. Birds started to sing, and were joined by the long, floating notes of the gibbons until the cool morning air was alive with sound.

For trees, pollination is only the beginning of the story. Once their flowers have been fertilised

66

and the petals have fallen away, the ovary is left to develop into a fruit that holds the seeds of a new generation. Here, trees face two problems. The first is that seeds are nutritious, and a favourite food of many animals. To overcome this, trees may cover them in protective cases or lace them with toxins or produce a vast number of seeds. Alternatively, they just produce a great deal of them. The extraordinary phenomenon of masting is a strategy to counter seed predation, according to Lisa Curran a Tropical Ecologist from the University of Michigan. She says that a clue to this may lie in the fact that during masting, even if blooming is slightly staggered, all the trees wait and drop their seeds at the same time. In a typical six-week masting period Lisa's research team collected 180 pounds of seeds ranging in size from a pistachio to a chestnut. 'It's like Thanksgiving in the forest,' she says.

Because so much seed is produced simultaneously over such a large area, there is a glut — a crop far greater than forest animals can eat — so there are still enough seeds left over to germinate and produce a carpet of new seedlings on the forest floor. The importance of this strategy has been highlighted by a recent article in *Science* where Lisa and her colleagues report that climate change and increasingly frequent occurrences of El Niño may be changing masting cycles, triggering trees to flower more frequently when they do not have the resources to produce many seeds. This, coupled with deforestation which concentrates animals in ever smaller areas, means that the survival of seeds is dramatically reduced. For instance, during a major fruiting at her study site during the 1998 El Niño year, no new dipterocarp seedings were found in the survey area.

However, even if the seeds are safe from predators, they cannot just fall to the ground and germinate: if they did, they would be in competition with the parent tree for light and nutrients. Instead, they must be dispersed, which presents trees with their second problem: they are rooted in the ground, unable to move, and need help to achieve this. The simplest method is to provide the seed with a parachute and let the wind do the rest. Balsa tree seeds are encased in fluffy pods, the seeds attached to fine hairs that are carried by the slightest breeze. Dipterocarp seeds have propellers to keep them airborne. But there are drawbacks to wind dispersal. Below the canopy there is little wind, so the seeds don't travel far. Also anything that relies on the wind to carry it has to be light: the seedlings of wind-dispersed plants lack a large, nutritious seed at their base to keep them alive in their early days of growth. Therefore, some trees once again enlist the help of animals. The trick is to get the animal to carry the seed without damaging it. Animals eat fruit, carry the seeds in their stomachs and scatter them through the forest. But many animals not only eat the fruit but the seeds too, and those that leave the seeds intact may deliver them to the wrong place. To avoid these problems some trees produce 'designer fruit' specifically to recruit a select band of animal couriers. The fruit is often large and gaudy, loaded with essential fats and proteins that provide a complete diet but can only be reached and carried by birds with a wide gape, such as hornbills. They swallow the fruit whole, then deposit the seeds over a huge area, with a rich fertiliser of manure. This method may sound reliable, but the trees that use it have to invest a lot of resources on each seed.

Another group of trees waits until after dark to offer up its fruits. They are often dull and muted in colour, but highly scented, and reliant on fruit bats to disperse the seeds. The pungent aroma of the durian is designed to draw in bats from miles around. A third group of trees invites everyone in the forest to an open buffet of fruit that contains countless seeds in the hope that some will fall on fertile ground. By far the most important of these are figs.

The following day, our last in Khao Yai, we found a gigantic fig tree. The ground around it was strewn with bright orangy-red fruit, some intact, some squashed and spilling out millions of tiny seeds. The unmistakable smell of ripe figs accosts you in rainforests across the world, and they are eaten by as many as 860 different species of bird and 240 mammals.

Figs are fantastically versatile: they can be creepers, climbers, shrubs, trees or epiphytes, and number about a thousand species. Larger trees fruit up to three times a year, with the ripe fruit remaining on them for several weeks, and the one we stood under would provide hornbills, mynah birds, fairy bluebirds, bulbuls, green pigeons, parrots, monitor lizards, squirrels, gibbons, macaques, civets, binturongs and even bears with fig banquets nearly all year round.

The tree before us was a majestic Benjamin fig, one of the most prolific of all fig trees, offering up some 25 kilos of fruit every day. During the fruiting season it produces 15 million seeds, to be carried away by a host of different animals. These trees are the mainstay of the forest, but they have a sinister side: they grow at the expense of other trees and belong to a group of trees known as strangler figs or in South America, *Matapalo*, the 'tree-killer'.

The strangler fig begins its life as a small, sticky seed deposited, usually by birds and bats, in the crook of a branch or in an epiphyte garden. It looks innocent as it grows into a small sapling but once it has gained a foothold it is only a matter of time before the host tree is overcome. This tiny plant gradually grows aerial roots, which eventually reach the forest floor and wrap round the massive trunk of its host. The fig taps into the tree's nutrient and water supply, rapidly thickening its roots and strengthening its hold on its victim, which becomes unable to expand its trunk and grow. High above, the fig's leaves are perfectly placed to soak up sunshine, spreading to shade the host tree's crown. The host, starved at both base and crown, dies and rots away, leaving a hollow core. The strangler fig continues to grow, and is now standing on thick roots of its own in the soil.

We were at the end of our stay in Thailand. I

had already climbed 45 metres up into the canopy; I had slept up in the canopy for several nights; now I was going to discover a tree from the inside out.

The fig tree was like a gigantic sculpture, a lattice of interwoven roots fused together to form a hollow tower. I climbed up inside the living cage. It was dingy and in places quite narrow. A cobweb brushed my face as I reached upwards, my hands and feet searching for holds among the nooks and crannies. Many creatures had probably made their homes there — geckos, frogs, anolis lizards, ants, beetles, spiders, cockroaches and paper wasps. The dark crevices were also perfect hiding-places for snakes. Dust hung in the shadowy tunnel below me, but a little way up light filtered through a few small chinks, illuminating the sinuous plexus of roots like gross intestines — it was as if I was in the belly of a giant monster.

Higher still a 'window' looked out over the forest below. I was about 25 metres up, cocooned inside a tree. Six metres further on, I emerged, blinking, into bright sunlight. From this vantage-point I surveyed the canopy and felt awed by the incredible strategy that had enabled this tree to take its place among the giants of the forest. It had killed its host, but now provided a valuable food supply and countless homes to forest residents. It was an embodiment of the cycles of life and death that create the richness of a rainforest.

4

The Cloud Forest

'Have you ever seen rain like this?' Mark shouted, above the sheets of rain hammering on the vegetation around us. We couldn't see further than a metre or so, our cotton shirts were stuck to our skins and water ran in rivulets off the ends of our noses. The path we were standing on had become a stream, and the reddish-brown earth had turned to mud. A flash of lightning lit up the trees and three seconds later thunder boomed around the valley. Mark was our director on this shoot and was taking it all in his stride. It had rained solidly for two days and didn't seem to be in any hurry to let up. We were in the Amazon and it was living up to its name as a rainforest.

Rain is the sprinkler system of the forest and essential to the variety of life that exists there. In most habitats, rainfall is measured in millimetres or centimetres but in the Amazon it is recorded in metres. The Amazon Basin is ringed by mountain ranges: to the south lies the Brazilian shield, to the north the Venezuelan Tepuis, the oldest mountains in the world, and stretching along the western edge, from Panama to Tierra del Fuego, the Andes.

We had started our journey to the Amazon a week or so earlier, flying from Lima, the capital of Peru, to Cuzco, high in the Andes. Beneath us the high peaks were sharp and rugged, indicating their 'recent' origin: a mere 20 million years old, they have not yet been worn smooth by the elements. Among the Pacific Ring of Fire, they were forced by tectonic activity to heights of up to 6000 metres. Only the Himalayas can boast a greater stature.

Even the land immediately below me spoke of recent turbulence in the earth: exposed layers of rock formed jagged crowns on top of the tawny-brown hills. The land stretched away into the distance, the muted colours broken occasionally by the grey-green lakes that glinted like jewels in deep valleys. It was harsh, dry country. The high *puna*, a cold alpine grassland covered in tussock grasses, certainly didn't appear to receive much rain. To the south lies the *altiplano*, the highest desert in the world. To the west, a thin strip of arid coastline stretches down to the Atacama desert in Chile, and Calama, the driest place on earth, where no rain had been recorded until 1998.

But to the east lay the vast richness of the Amazon jungle. It seemed a world away, yet these barren mountains are essential to its existence. The puffy white clouds I could see from the plane window provided the link. As warm air from the Amazon Basin plains hits the gigantic wall of the Andes, it is forced upwards. As it rises it cools. Then the moisture it carries condenses, forming heavy clouds, and falls as rain or, at higher elevations, as snow. Because the Andes are so steep, the air is forced up abruptly so the moisture condenses quickly, falls as heavy rain on the eastern slopes and pours back into the Amazon Basin. In a phenomenon known as the 'rain shadow' effect, the air that eventually passes over the mountains is essentially depleted of moisture, producing the dry deserts to the west.

Cuzco, the ancient capital of the Incas and still a bustling town, is situated at 3,400 metres in the Peruvian Andes. From here we planned to travel first by road over the crest of the mountains to the headwaters of the Madre de Dios river, then down through the cloud forest till we reached the Pilcopata, a major tributary of the Madre de Dios. Where the Pilcopata becomes navigable we would take to the river on rafts and descend through the foothills of the Andes and into the Amazon Basin.

From Cuzco a winding road took us south-east, climbing steadily towards snowy peaks. The slopes around us were pale brown, dotted with sparse vegetation. There were signs of cultivation in only a few river valleys, often no more than the odd patch of maize. Small wooden houses were clustered along the road, their tiled roofs adorned with pairs of terracotta bulls to bring their occupants prosperity and fertility. The Quechua who live here are descendants of the Incas, beautiful mountain people who bring colour to the landscape with the bright reds, pinks, oranges and yellows of their clothes and pointy hats. Even their llamas and alpacas wear red and orange, in the tassels that hang from their ears.

From the back seat of our mini bus, Jake gave us a quick lesson in how to distinguish the llama from the alpaca. 'Llama,' he said, pulling his face into a pout, with raised eyebrows and an imperious expression, then 'Alpaca,' pushing his mouth into a dainty little pucker and blinking widely. It was a perfect mime of the animal's benign but vacant expression.

Llamas and alpacas are essential to life in this region: they are beasts of burden but also provide wool, milk and meat, and their pretty ear tassels show that they are cherished — but, then, so are other animals: we saw a dog padding along the road in a tattered navy blue jumper to keep out the cold.

It appeared to be a rural idyll, but as I looked out at the dry hillsides I knew it must be a tough existence and I wondered how this land could ever have supported a thriving Inca city. We continued east and soon I had my answer. We rounded a corner to a panorama of snowcapped mountains stretching across the head of a wide, sweeping valley. This is Wilcamayu, the sacred valley of the Incas, rich, fertile and watered by the wide, winding river. Many of the crops that the Quechua grow are the same as those grown by their forebears — various species of corn and a staggering range of potatoes. This is the home of the potato and there are literally hundreds of kinds to be found here. We stopped to stretch our legs in Pocatamba, a picturesque little town built in a Spanish colonial style with a stone bridge crossing the river and an immaculate square surrounded by smart houses with smart blue shutters. At a vegetable stall we marvelled at potatoes — some brilliant yellow or red, some marbled red and white like raspberry ripple ice-cream, others long, brown and knobbly, like chunky Twiglets.

Our destination that night was a place called Tres Cruxes, some 3,500 metres up on the eastern edge of the Andes. We arrived just after dark and set up our tents. We felt breathless in the thin air and it was bitingly cold — we were glad of the extra woollies we had bought in Cuzco, alpaca gloves, hats and jumpers. Against the clear sky, the stars dazzled in such profusion that familiar constellations looked quite different. It took me a long time to fall asleep, as I lay listening to the wind and thinking about the journey ahead of us. It had been my childhood dream to explore the Amazon and now I was on its doorstep.

When we woke it was still dark, the constellation of Orion hanging low over the horizon. I pulled on a thick fleece, alpaca hat and gloves. I cradled a mug of coffee as I watched the stars fade and the landscape gain definition. The previous night we had had no inkling of the sight that awaited us in the morning. Now, with no higher point between me and the Atlantic Ocean, 2,000 miles away, I had an unimpeded view as the sun rose across a continent.

The contrast with the barren landscape we had flown over the day before could not have been more dramatic. The steep slopes were covered with lush vegetation and way below, stretching as far as I could see, was the Amazon Basin and the largest rainforest on earth. Covering an area of 7.5 million square kilometres, the Amazon jungle has the greatest genetic diversity of life on earth: at least 2 million species of insect, 30,000 species of plant, 2,500 species of fish, 950 species of bird, and 500 species of mammal, including the world's largest number of different species of monkeys. In a land of superlatives it can be hard to get a sense of perspective, but that dawn at Tres Cruxes helped me to grasp the immensity of the forest that lay below and gave me a feeling for the spirit of the land.

There is something especially vital and energetic about this part of the world. You can't help but feel that here Mother Nature — 'Pacha Mama', as she is known locally — has given her all. As Darwin wrote, 'The land is one great wild, untidy luxuriant hothouse made by Nature for herself.' A severe mountain of rock tinted red with the rising sun loomed above me. This was Apu Canyewaye, which means Lord of the Fire; it had been sacred to the Incas. It is one of the *apus*, or sentinels, that look out across the Amazon Basin, guarding Pacha Mama. I looked up at Apu Canyewaye and hoped it approved of our proposed journey.

Through wisps of cloud the mountain ridges tripped away from us, smaller and smaller until at last they flattened into the vast plain of the Amazon. Our journey was laid out before us. We could see the route we would take down through the mountains and there, glinting in the light, were the fast-flowing waters of the Pilcopata river that would carry us to the foot of the Andes, through the Konyec Canyon, and out into the Amazon. Beyond that, far in the distance, I could just make out the silvery thread of the Madre de Dios, which would take us deep into the rainforest. Out of sight, somewhere far to the north near the end of our journey, lay the mighty Amazon itself.

Up here, with my breath visible as little white puffs in the cold air, I felt far removed from the steamy jungle and its snaking rivers. It was bitterly cold, but we strolled over the ridge through the golden tussock grasses and club mosses that survive on these windswept moun-tainsides. Club mosses, with their delicate worm-like green fingers curling upwards, are primitive plants, the first stage between a moss and a fern. It struck me that our journey down to the Amazon would take us through a progression of vegetation that almost mirrored the evolution of plants, from the small and simple to the luxuriant 'hothouse' of the jungle.

From the *puna* grassland we glimpsed little copses through the floating mists, small clumps of stunted trees huddled close together in the shelter of steep ravines. It is known as 'elfin wood', and it was like an enchanted forest, or Tolkien's Middle Earth. The gnarled trees are barely two metres tall and heavily cloaked with pale wispy lichens and green algae. Velvety mosses of deep green, yellow, orange and red blanket their lower branches and twisted roots, and spread across the hummocky ground with such luxuriance that I could bury my whole hand in the soft, springy tissue.

The trees all look very similar and belong to just a few genera — *Podocarpus*, *Clusia* and *Gynoxys*. Despite the elfin wood's cosy appearance, trees do not have an easy life up here: the constant cold stunts their growth, while the perpetual mists that hang over the hillsides veil the sun and create an atmosphere so saturated with water that transpiration, a process in which evaporation from leaves enables plants to draw up water and nutrients from the soil, is restricted.

Later we drove down the eastern slopes of the Andes, the minibus groaning with gear and people. Along with Si, Jake, Mark and myself was our production coordinator, Rita, and our guide, Roberto, who was from Cuzco. He was not your average guide — a silver ring through his right eyebrow, a woolly hat pulled down over his head and a massive smile on his face. He was both very knowledgeable and enthusiastic about his country. As we rounded a corner he pointed out a trail by the side of the road. It had been made five hundred years ago by the Spanish to transport sugar-cane and coca from the Amazon

Basin up to Cuzco. The mountains are very steep so it must have been quite a climb. Roberto told us he had walked it three times — 'Well . . . I've actually walked down it three times and got a lift back up to Cuzco by car,' he said. 'But it's amazing, like going back in history.' Apparently the path takes you down ancient steps that have been carved in rock and worn smooth by feet and donkey hoofs.

The views were breathtaking and hair-raising in equal measure. The road clung to the sheer mountainside and at each sharp bend the front of the minibus swept across a precipice that plummeted more than a thousand metres to a foaming white river below. Above us, the tops of the hills were wreathed in mist, with fingers of cloud reaching down into the ravines, and waterfalls spilling down a thousand metres from the cliffs. The air smelt damp and spicy. It was getting warmer and the light less diffuse. Suddenly the vegetation had gone mad. We had entered the cloud forest.

One of the reasons why the Amazon supports such a diversity of species is that there are distinct vegetation zones according to elevation. Here, the trees were much taller, 25–30 metres, their branches covered with dark mosses and pale wispy lichens, and festooned with ferns, bromeliads and orchids. Tree ferns like *Cyathea* stood in the shadows under this luxuriant awning, adding to the mysterious, primeval appearance of the forest. The exceptional number of epiphytes found here is the result of the blanket of moist cloud that constantly bathes the canopy. Epiphytes live on other plants, but while many orchids, ferns and bromeliads flourish in the branches of tall trees, the problem they face in forests around the world is getting enough water because unlike other plants, they cannot tap this directly from the ground. As you descend from the cloud forest to a warmer drier climate the number of epiphytes declines rapidly; at lower altitudes many are cacti with fat succulent leaves, but the cloud forest is the wettest forest on earth and bromeliads, in particular, are everywhere, arranged neatly along the branches that stretch out over steep ravines.

Bromeliads are high-rise relatives of the pineapple, with spiky crowns of leaves ranging from pinkish brown to dark green or deep burgundy. They are important to many of the animals that live here. This is the home of Paddington Bear's relatives. Spectacled bears live here in the cloud forest and feast on bromeliad hearts, but I knew I was unlikely to see one. Although they once ranged from the southern United States right through Central and South America, this is their last refuge and they are now rare due to hunting and loss of habitat.

The inner leaves of tank bromeliads are arranged to form a receptacle that catches rainwater, offering drinking pools for spectacled bears, coatis, monkeys, sloths and other animals. They are also luxurious roof top pools for a variety of smaller creatures, creating little water worlds in tree tops. Swimming around in them are waterbeetles and the larvae of mosquitoes, midges and dragonflies. Several species of tree frog and poison dart frog also use them as nurseries.

Male poison dart frogs fight for the right to occupy a pool, as males that own swimming pools get the females. Some species carry eggs on their backs and when they hatch they release the tadpoles in the water, while others continue to carry their tadpoles and only leave them in pools when they have developed into tiny frogs. One poison-dart frog female deposits a single tadpole in each pole, avoiding those that are already occupied by tadpoles of her species. If the pool is occupied the resident tadpole signals to her, telling her to get lost by shaking its tail. Once she has all her tadpoles satisfactorily ensconced in their nursery pools she returns to visit each one in turn, and leaves them with an unfertilized egg as food.

These pools are not always quiet sanctuaries. Vine snakes stake out the pools to catch tree frogs, but the poison dart frogs and their offspring are usually left well alone. They tend to be highly colourful characters, some with luminous green stripes, others are pale blue with black leopard spots and red heads. My favourite is the strawberry poison dart frog, which is found in the Atlantic lowland tropical forests of Central America and has a scarlet body and purple legs. These attractive colours though, are a dire warning: their skin secretes toxic alkaloids that can block neural transmission causing convulsions, paralysis and eventually death. This lethal defense system can be transferred to their offspring while these are carried around on their backs.

The poison of some of these frogs can be strong enough to kill a monkey and it can cause serious neurological damage to humans. However, their powerful weapon is a double-edged sword: far from saving the frogs, the secretions have made them a target. The effectiveness of the neurotoxins was discovered long ago by Choco Indians who collect the frogs to poison their blowpipe darts.

Among the overgrown tangle of green, the cloud forest is full of vibrant colour. The brilliant orange and yellow slipper flowers, red begonias and fuchsias, lurid pink anthuriams and pale pink crucifix orchids are a visual magnet for birds and insects. Many of these species are familiar in our own living rooms or gardens — but these were giants. The begonias stood about 2.5 metres tall their fat stems covered in a soft fur of deep red hairs. The fiery bracts of crab-claw heliconias attracted iridescent hummingbirds. I glimpsed one hovering at a flower, shimmering green and indigo among the red flowers, its wings a blur as they beat some 80 times a second in order to hang motionless in the air. Its long, down-turned bill was perfectly designed to drink deeply of the sticky nectar that oozes from within the little flowers. The nectar of heliconias is an important food for many kinds of hummingbirds, but their fruits are also prized by other forest birds. At one study site in Costa Rica as many as twenty-eight species of birds were observed feeding on one species of heliconia. In return for their meal, the birds help disperse the seeds, digesting the pulp and regurgitating the seed whole. Heliconias are great opportunists. Closely related to bananas, their large paddle-shaped leaves are thirsty for sunlight and sometimes whole 'plantations' of heliconias quickly move in when the fall of a tree has allowed light through to ground level.

The road was also bordered by many tall thin Cecropia trees, with deeply-lobed, palmate leaves hanging like small parasols from the top of their spindly trunks. These trees are highly effective colonisers and have much in common with their fellow pioneers, the Macaranga trees of South East Asia. As with Macaranga trees, Cecropia are pole-like but they are also hollow inside, presumably a further adaptation allowing them to devote energy to growing at speeds of about two and a half metres a year. The hollow cavities provide particularly spacious apartments for their residents, because like Macaranga trees they employ ants, in their case Azteca ants, as body guards.

As we drove along I kept a close look out for pale shapes hanging from the branches. Cecropia leaves are a favourite food of the three-toed sloth. Sloths are somewhat comic creatures, most closely related to armadillos and anteaters, with shaggy hair, long arms and legs and sweet round faces with vacuous expressions. There are six to seven species represented by two distinct groups: the three-toed sloth and the two-toed sloth, and all of them live in the canopy where they subsist on leaves. Despite the huge abundance of canopy leaves, few mammals are properly equipped to eat them because cellulose is difficult to digest. In order to cope, sloths have stomachs that are divided into many digestive compartments and contain cellulose-digesting bacteria. But even so the leaves can take up to a month to digest and so they have a very sluggish lifestyle, with minimum movement and about fifteen hours a day of sleep.

If you happen to see one in a tree you can rest assured that you will have plenty of time to look at it. As John Kricher says in *A Neotropical Companion*. 'If you care to watch a sloth move from one tree to another, a distance that would take a few seconds for a monkey, plan to spend about a day or so.'

Sloths spend most of their time hanging from branches upside down and to facilitate water runoff the hair of both species grows from the stomach to the back. Even so, such is the torpor of these animals there is time for algae to grow in their fur giving it a greenish tinge that helps to camouflage it from predators like the harpy eagle. In fact the sloth's fur is an entire ecosystem of its own: one study found more than 950 beetles living off the algae on a single sloth.

Once a week sloths make an arduous journey to the base of their tree to do their business. They could easily defecate from up in the branches so why do they put themselves at risk to terrestrial predators? The answer may be that because sloths rely on a limited number of Cecropia trees to feed them they make an effort to look after them. By defecating at the base of their host tree they ensure it gets precious fertilizer, a rare but vital commodity in most rainforests.

Despite keeping our eyes peeled, none were to be seen. Here and there a tree was hung with pendulous nests from which oropendulas, a glamorous relative of the blackbird, flew in and out, with flashes of yellow as their tails fanned out against the sky. Every now and then I glimpsed one of the technicolour tanagers: the silver-beaked, with its deep rufous chest, the yellow-bellied, with cap to match, and the paradise tanager, dazzling with its iridescent turquoise breast, green head and scarlet rump. Most startling of all was the cock-of-the-rock, a rotund, vivid orange bird that stood out like a beacon in the valleys by the streams.

Given that the cloud forest is drenched with 10 metres of water a year and is on such a steep gradient, you might expect this to be landslide country, but it is not: the forest's roots hold on to the waterlogged soils, so that the water, rather than pouring down the hillsides taking the topsoil with it, seeps out gradually — the ground was so soggy underfoot that it was like tramping across a bog (there was even sphagnum moss, as there is in moorlands and bogs in Britain). And this is what makes the cloud forest so important: by absorbing water and trapping it in the soil, it acts like a gigantic sponge, collecting water and releasing it gradually into the Amazon Basin. We know now that the fresh-water supplies of the earth depend on healthy forests and their loss will not only damage the environment but threaten the lives of millions of people.

Water is the most precious substance on earth. It is essential to all life and the first thing we look for when we search for life on other planets. In its liquid state it is a perfect carrier, either for transporting molecules inside plants, animals and humans, allowing our vital systems to function, or moving substances such as minerals and organic compounds around the earth, changing the environment and driving many different lifecycles.

Everywhere around us beads of water clung to the tips of mosses. Sometimes, where clumps overhung a bank of rock, the beads formed a steady drip and tiny trickles glinted against the stone. On these steep hillsides there is only one way for water to go and that is straight down: as it moves, trickles join other trickles gradually growing into rivulets and streams, which cascade down the mountains, eroding the rocks, picking up a cargo of minerals and carrying it along the rivers and, eventually, into the Amazon.

As we descended to the lower slopes it got steadily warmer. The cloud forest was giving way to palms and tall broad-leafed trees with fewer epiphytes. It was beginning to look more like tropical rainforest. Once, when we had stopped *en route* to film, Roberto pointed out a flattened snake in the road. It was small and dead, but he treated it with the utmost caution: it was a fer-de-lance, one of the most poisonous snakes in the world. He opened its mouth with a stick: 'Check out those teeth — you don't want them puncturing your skin,' he said, pointing at the large fangs at the front of its mouth. Its scientific name is *Lachesis*, after one of the three Fates in Greek mythology, who measured the length of the thread of life. It was a fantastic opportunity to study this renowned snake but, as it turned out, it wasn't the last time we'd meet a fer-de-lance, and the next one was very much alive.

A little later we said goodbye to our minibus and driver. From now on our best route was by water, but what had once been placid streams had become turbulent rivers. It was time to don lifejackets. We were to travel the rest of the way by raft, riding the white water through the last folds of the Andes into the planes below. We met up with our rafting team, a lively crew of Peruvians who were skilled at navigating these waters.

'Bestia!' Antonio shouted. He was talking to Piero, a Goliath of a man they had nicknamed 'the Beast'. The rafts had to be loaded on to a tractor in order to get them down the muddy track that led to the river, and Bestia's strength was required. After much shouting, haranguing and laughter, the rafts were in the river, and we were away, racing through crystal-clear waters, dancing and twirling in the current.

We sped between the huge boulders that littered the river to shouts of 'Forward! Forward left!' and 'Back! Back now!' Pepe was the team leader: he searched the river ahead and issued the commands. We responded in unison, pulling on our paddles for all we were worth, or heaving back on them to slow the raft and slip round a rock.

Torrents of water crashed over us and it was impossible to keep anything dry. The radio microphone transmitter I was wearing was in a splashproof case but Jake had fixed me with a stern look and said, 'Try to keep it as dry as possible.' He wasn't sure he could trust me since I had jumped in the river to cool off earlier, forgetting that I was still wearing his transmitter. Almost everything had been stowed away in waterproof cases and tied down, except for a video camera in a splash bag that Si was using to film the action. Wedged down in the front of the raft, facing backwards, he was holding on with one hand and operating the camera with the other when the inevitable happened. We came down an especially violent set of rapids and the raft lurched to one side. 'Back!' shouted Pepe. At that moment we crashed against a rock and the raft lifted out of the water, sending us all tumbling into each other and several thousand pounds' worth of camera spiralling into the foaming white water of the Pilcopata. Si went straight in after it. 'Si!' shouted Pepe, but Bestia had already grabbed Si's arm. We paddled furiously to control the raft in the violent current as Bestia struggled to haul him out. A few minutes later Si rejoined us, on the raft triumphantly clutching the camera.

Gradually the swirling waters calmed and the river grew steadily wider as it was joined by more and more tributaries. About thirty kilometres downstream we were passing fields on the banks and children ran along the shore waving to us as we rowed into the small town of Pilcopata. The Villa Carmen was a good place to get dry. It was just outside the town, an old Spanish-style hacienda and working farm, with crops, cattle and horses as well as a menagerie of rescued animals — sloths, peccaries and a scarlet macaw called Bandito — who had been left homeless when areas of forest were cleared.

The following day we would continue our journey downriver and finally enter the Amazon, but for now the Villa Carmen, with its happy chaos and large kitchen, was the perfect place to refuel and dry off. The camera was placed in Intensive Care — Si nursed it with Rita's hair-dryer. A hair-dryer might not be the first thing you'd think to bring on a trip to the Amazon but it proved its unique value in the rainforest many times over.

Greta ran the farm with her husband and seemed undaunted by the large number of people she had to feed. Afterwards, we sat around chatting in the friendly atmosphere. It was our last night together: we would part company with the rafting crew the following afternoon and with Roberto soon after that. We raised several toasts, and splashed a little beer on the ground, the customary offering to Pacha Mama.

Roberto produced a book of photographs depicting the wildlife of Manu National Park, which was where we were heading next. 'You're going to love it,' he said, as we flicked through many stunning images of animals including giant otters and colourful macaws. Every page revealed an extraordinary animal, insect or plant but what struck me most was the number of captions that read, 'Species unknown.' We were about to enter one of the last great wildernesses on earth.

While almost every corner of the globe has been explored there is still a great deal we do not know about the Amazon rainforest. One man has probably contributed to our knowledge of the Amazon more than any: Alexander von Humboldt. With his friend, the French medical doctor and botanist Aime-Jacques-Alexandre Goujoud Bonpland, he was the first European to explore much of Central and South America in series of expeditions over five years from 1799 to 1804, which took them through Venezuela and much of Peru, Ecuador, Colombia and Mexico.

But they did much more than explore. They were men with an extraordinary breadth of interests and actively enquiring minds. On their many expeditions they recorded and collected plant, animal, and mineral specimens, discovering for the first time an animal that can produce electricity, the electric eel. They also conducted extensive mapping of northern South America, climbed mountains, set altitude records and observed astronomical phenomena.

He has been a source of inspiration for generations of naturalists and scientists, among them Charles Darwin. When Darwin set out on his historic voyage on the *Beagle* thirty-seven years later, he travelled with a translation on board of Humboldt's *Personal Narrative*, from which he memorized entire passages by heart.

What makes Humboldt particularly special was the universality of his outlook. He always strived to look at the whole picture and anticipated the modern study of ecosystems. He once wrote ... 'the aims I strive for are an understanding of nature as a whole, proof of the working together of all the forces of nature.' There is nowhere where this is more evident than tropical rainforests.

Next morning we woke early. Mark was up first and was startled to hear to hear a cheery 'Hola,' as there wasn't a soul around. It took him a few moments to realise he had been greeted by Bandito, the macaw, who habitually slept on top of the door. The rest of us were greeted in similar fashion as we emerged which was decent of him as the poor bird must have been swung back and forth on his perch innumerable times with the traffic to the out house during the night.

An hour later we said 'Hasta la vista' to all at Villa Carmen, including Bandito, and were soon back on the Pilcopata river. Shortly afterwards, the Pilcopata was joined by the Toño and the Piñipiñi, and opened up to become a wide channel of swirling, pale brown water. Ahead were the low ridge of the Pinipini mountains, the final barrier before the Amazon Basin. The sky was dark behind the towering shapes of the Andes, and we could see back to where we had camped up at Tres Cruxes.

It was late afternoon when we reached Koñec Canyon, the final gateway into the Amazon Basin. Steep cliffs rose above us on either side, like great portals and as we paddled between them the sky grew ominously dark, distant thunder rolled over the hills and we felt the first spots of rain. It was a suitably theatrical entrance into the Amazon.

The following day we went up to a lookout tower at the top of a hill for a view over the canopy. Even though there was a glimmer of light in the sky, under the eaves of the forest it was still dark. We trudged up the steep hill in silence, our torch-beams forming a string of flickering lights through the trees. The air was heavy and we could hear the soft, almost imperceptible, sound of water dripping from the leaves around us. It smelt rich and damp, and on the ground the dead leaves made a soft, springy 'scrunch . . . scrunch' underfoot. A call rang out through the forest: a clear series of notes descending in pitch, 'Do . . . do-do-do.' Moments later it was repeated, then again. 'Do . . . do-do-do.' I was thrilled — it was a potoo, a bird that's not easy to meet. This relative of the nightjar goes abroad at night but at dawn it settles down to sleep disguising itself perfectly as a dead branch.

We had been going for about forty minutes, with Salvatore, our local guide, leading the way, followed by Si, me, Rita, Roberto and Mark. Jake was not with us as he had succumbed to a stomach bug. I was only a pace behind Si, the batteries of my torch were dying and so I was following his light. I watched his boots as he walked. Then my eyes flicked to the edge of the path, just centimetres from where his boot had come down. I sprang back with a cry. 'There's a snake right here in front of me on the path — I'm not moving!'

Rita and Mark had stopped behind me and swung their torch beams to where I was pointing. Roberto came hurrying up. 'Do you know what it is?' I asked.

Our torches had revealed a two-tone brown snake with a faint white pattern that perfectly disguised it in the leaf litter. It was tightly coiled but its head was raised and its tongue flicked in and out.

'My God!' Robert said. 'It's a fer-de-lance — a *huge* one. The biggest I've seen. You're lucky you saw it — it looks ready to strike.'

The fer-de-lance is a classic ambush predator. It sits on a suitable trail and waits, sometimes for weeks, until prey wanders into its range. It would certainly have picked up the vibrations we had made as we walked through the forest, and although it would have regarded us an unsuitably large prey, it probably felt uneasy with us walking past.

'Where are Si and Salvatore?' Roberto asked.

'They walked straight past it,' I told him.

The snake was now searching the air with its tongue, obviously aware that it was the centre of attention. It swayed its head gently from side to side as it began to uncoil and move across the path. Roberto took a step closer for a better look, but the rest of us stood absolutely still as it slid slowly over the edge of the path and down the hill. Fer-de-lances can grow to about four metres long, but this one looked quite big enough at about 2.5 metres! Still, there's nothing like a surge of adrenaline to wake you up in the morning, and we continued on our way feeling somewhat more alert.

When we climbed up the metal observation tower, an extraordinary sight greeted us. The first rays of sun sent beams of light through the mists that were rising up from the canopy and spiralling into the sky: water vapour produced by the trees. During the day the sun evaporates water from the leaves creating a pump action in which the tree pulls water up from its roots. Each tree draws up hundreds of gallons each day from the ground but it uses only a small amount of this. The rest is released into the atmosphere at night, along with oxygen, through tiny pores in the leaves, a process known as transpiration. It is almost as if they are breathing out. At dawn the warm moist air that has been trapped among the trees rises towards the cooler air above and condenses into swirling mists. We were watching one of the most powerful processes on the planet. The trees of the Amazon lift 8 billion tonnes of water into the atmosphere every year. The artificial energy that would be required to do this is estimated to be the equivalent of half a million atomic bombs exploding each day.

Once the vapour has been released, prevailing winds carry it across the forest, picking up more and more until the air is saturated and the water falls again as rain. The Amazon is so large that it creates its own weather system: half of the rain that falls here is produced by the trees themselves and by drawing up water from the ground then passing it through the atmosphere the forest acts like a huge rain conveyor-belt, a sort of giant Mexican wave all the way from the Atlantic to the Andes. As it passes through the canopy, the composition of the water changes slightly: it absorbs soluble organic compounds leached from leaves, stems, branches and trunks, and so has a much higher concentration of minerals, compounds that are essential to plant growth, than the original rain. One droplet of water can take a remarkable voyage: it might be recycled through dozens of trees, passing on minerals at each stage, and travel nearly 3000 kilometres before it reaches the Andes. Here it is carried high into the mountains where it cools abruptly and falls as snow or rain, then spills back into the Amazon Basin in a river. The forest makes rain and the Andes keep recycling within the Amazon Basin.

Within an hour the mist began to disperse in the warmth of the sun's rays. As the morning progressed the warm air currents over the canopy picked up more and more moisture until the air was saturated and great clouds unfolded in the sky announcing an afternoon of thunder and rain.

5

Rivers of Life

The colossal quantities of rain that fall in rainforests feed the huge river systems that carve their way through them. We continued our journey into the Amazon Basin on the Madre de Dios river. The coffee-coloured water spraying out from under the prow of our motorised canoe was clearly heavily laden with sediment, nutrients and minerals washed down from the Andes. These rivers are not only the means by which people get around, they are also the lifeblood of the Amazon, like arteries, nourishing the forest.

Travelling on the Madre de Dios was a considerably calmer experience than our last river journey on the Pilcopata had been. Walter, who was leading on this leg of the journey, was not your usual rufty-tufty jungle guide. Small and slightly portly, he always wore a freshly pressed shirt and a sleeveless khaki bush jacket that on him somehow looked like a smart waistcoat. His motorised canoe was well appointed too, with a plastic awning to shade us from the sun, and comfortable seats.

The lives of many animals in the Amazon Basin revolve around its rivers. We passed a regal-looking bird, a great black hawk, strutting along the edge of the water. The striking white patch on its lower wing stood out against the rest of its shiny plumage, and the yellow trim on its tail matched its legs. A trio of side-neck turtles sat companionably on a dead tree sunning themselves, butterflies sipping at their tears for the salts. A little further on, a group of capybaras, grazing on the grassy bank, eyed us suspiciously as our boat approached. Capybaras are the largest rodents in the world: they look rather like guinea pigs but are the size of a domestic pig. One of the females had a youngster feeding alongside her and gave a staccato bark as if to warn us off.

Many of the trees that bordered the river were in flower: the red velvety blooms of a species of *Combretum*, polina trees, thickly covered in an abundance of fluffy golden brown flowers; and another specimen, whose pale speckled bark and delicate, dusty pink flowers reminded me of the blossom trees in a Japanese painting. Ahead, in the bend of the river stood a massive ceiba or kapok tree, sacred to the local people. Its scale struck me: it was very big in comparison with the other trees. I had expected that the Amazon would be full of vast ones but much of the forest along the banks had looked a bit straggly and lacked a sense of permanence. We were about to discover why.

As we rounded a bend an apocalyptic sight greeted us. All around us massive trees lay dead in the water, bleached white like the skeletons of dinosaurs. Although so much of life in the forest revolves around these rivers, they also destroy. The Madre de Dios seemed calm now, but after heavy rains it became tempestuous, bursting its banks, uprooting giant trees and sweeping everything in its path. This was the aftermath of such an event.

We continued cautiously downstream, our boatman carefully navigating through the tree-trunks that littered the water. We came across an enormous ceiba lying on its side in the river, with flaring buttress roots. I climbed out of the boat and sat on one, dwarfed by its size. 'It looks like a crashed space rocket,' said Mark.

'There is a legend that the ceiba is the mother of the Amazon,' Walter said. 'The story goes that a huge ancient ceiba fell and its branches became the tributaries of the Amazon and the trunk the river itself. The leaves turned into canoes to transport people along the waterways.'

As we weaved our way through the carnage in the river, Walter told us that the rising river brought his village extraordinary wealth — giant uprooted trees worth thousands of dollars come floating down the river and all they have to do is catch them. 'It's a kind of tradition', he said, 'we all go out in small canoes, about twenty canoes all work together to try and catch the tree with a rope and drag it to shore.'

It must be total mayhem. Twenty canoes with two people apiece makes up just one team, and there can be several teams out at the same time bobbing about in the churning water while trying to lasso the trees as they come racing down the river. Canoes sometimes capsize but despite the apparent chaos they do adhere to some kind of etiquette. No one can be quite sure when the river will rise — it could be day or night — but when it does the quickest people to put their names down on the list can lay claim to the first, second and third logs to come down. But it's a lottery as there is no way of telling what logs the river will bring. Apparently, you can pass up on the first log but then you must take the second, which may not be as good. Then the second and third claimants get their logs and after that it develops into a free-for-all, and the first canoe that reaches the log can claim it. A cedar can be worth $1000 and a mahogany considerably more so; even if the profits are shared between 40 people there is serious money to be made.

It was late afternoon when we came to Walter's village, our first sign of habitation in more than six hours on the river. Boca Manu was not what you might expect of a village deep in the Amazon jungle: a newly painted sign on the bank welcomed us and beyond that neat wooden houses surrounded a village green — or, rather, football pitch. Gravelled paths lined with whitewashed stones and bordered by gay flowerbeds meandered between the houses, and at regular intervals green-painted litter bins were posted with signs requesting that rubbish be disposed of properly. By the football pitch there was even a neat row of public urinals constructed from palm fronds. 'People used to go anywhere when there was a football match in progress [as there usually was, I discovered]. Now everything is much more hygienic,' Walter said proudly.

Perhaps it shouldn't have been such a surprise — after all, Walter was the mayor of the village and he had decided it was time that Boca Manu pulled its socks up. The village had had a reputation for alcoholism and slovenliness: many of the villagers made a living by catching logs, and when the river was low they spent much of their time drinking beer and playing football. Walter had decided that things had to change, and the showpiece village was the result.

We could hear the sound of an engine at the top of the bank and a smart new tractor and trailer, holding most of the village children, appeared. They had come to help us unload our gear and take it to Walter's newly built visitors' lodge. As there were no roads for about 70 kilometres in every direction I wondered how on earth the tractor had reached Boca Manu.

'We brought it down the river like everything else,' Walter told us. 'We lashed two canoes together and perched it on top.'

Certainly it was the pride and joy of Boca

Manu and we all climbed aboard and drove to our sleeping quarters, even though they were only 150 metres away. The tractor driver reversed and then proceeded straight over a couple of flowerbeds and paths, knocking whitewashed stones out of alignment.

'Um, we seem to be causing a bit of damage,' Si said.

'It's no problem, no problem at all,' Walter said cheerfully as we crushed some red begonias. Obviously the tractor could do no wrong. Besides, it kept work in progress and — presumably — people away from the bar.

That night Walter took us out in the boat so that we could go for a swim in the river. 'You have to choose your spot carefully — avoid shallow sandy areas where there are stingrays and electric eels and banks where there are caimans,' he warned us. Stingrays in the Amazon can reach a metre across, while electric eels are equally gigantic and produce 800 volts of electricity, enough to stun a horse. Black caimans, closely related to alligators, can apparently swallow a man whole. Walter, though, had been swimming in the river since childhood and knew the safe areas. The strength of the current took me by surprise as I dived into the cool, invigorating water. I was glad that it was shallow enough for me to stand — I had to swim furiously to avoid being swept away. After about five minutes I had a new respect for the power of the river and could understand why sandbags were piled up against the bank in front of the village — Boca Manu was in permanent danger of being washed away.

While many plants, animals and human communities are destroyed by these turbulent rivers, this dynamic environment brings fantastic opportunities to others. The next leg of our journey took us to a place where the destructive force of water had created one of the Amazon's most amazing spectacles.

Close to the river a small airstrip had been cut into the forest. It didn't see much traffic at the moment — in fact, the Cessna we were waiting for was the only plane that landed there, about once a week. We had about half an hour before it was due to arrive and I laid out my damp laundry across the cases stacked at the edge of the airstrip in the hope that it might dry (drying clothes in the jungle is difficult and the opportunity to get some direct sun was not to be missed). We sat in the shade of the unprepossessing shack that was the 'airport terminal'. Jake and Si pored over motorcycle magazines while the others chatted, and I read my book.

Time passed, with no sign of the plane. Walter tried to contact the pilot by radio without success. Periodically we walked out on to the airstrip and checked the sky, then went back into the little wooden shack.

'It's bound to be here soon,' Walter said, but I wasn't so sure. I had spotted a note scratched into the bench I was sitting on which said, 'Waiting for plane 12/10/97'. Below it, days had been crossed off, eight in total. Another slightly desperate message simply read, '8 seats, 11 people . . . '

At last we heard the sound of our plane approaching. I grabbed my laundry which was now dry, and ten minutes later we were airborne. The Madre de Dios region is the least populated part of Peru and we flew over pristine forest for mile after mile, broken by meandering rivers and ox-bow lakes at every stage of development. Then the landscape changed abruptly: swathes of forest had been cut down, leaving dark brown scars, while in other places it had been burned, and charred remains of trees stood askew in the blackened earth. We were approaching Puerto Maldonado.

When we got out of the plane, the heat assaulted us like a punch in the face. But that was not the only thing: we'd been in the forest for a long time and suddenly we were in the middle of a hectic frontier town, with concrete buildings chaotically thrown together and the main street milling with motor-scooters. Puerto Maldonado has a population of about forty thousand timber traders, gold-miners, Brazil-nut merchants and farmers. We bought the supplies we needed as quickly as possible and headed out on a dirt road leading south towards Tambopata National Park. After about ten kilometres we transferred once again to boats on Tambopata River.

'Isn't Fitzcarraldo's boat somewhere along here?' Mark asked Guillermo, a biologist from Tambopata Research Centre who had come to meet us.

Fitzcarraldo was an eccentric rubber baron, who had dreamed of bringing high culture to the heart of the rainforest. He had wanted the famed opera singers Caruso and Bernhardt to perform Verdi in a town called Iquitos. The story goes that to finance his dream he had to exploit the vast rubber trees that grew beyond the Ucayali Falls. To pass this barrier, he had to get his 32-tonne steamboat from one branch of the river to another. With the help of a local tribe, and fighting fever, mosquitoes and suffocating heat, he had realized his dream.

'Yes, we've missed it, I'm afraid. It's just upstream from Puerto Maldonado. Now it's no longer in the river, though, but in the middle of the forest,' Guillermo said. I wondered if it had been left high and dry because of the movement of the river, which can suddenly change its course, swerving as much as seven kilometres.

That night we stayed in a lodge called Posada Amazonas, set up to cater for the wealthy tourists who fly in for a quick rainforest experience before continuing on to Machu Picchu and other Inca sites. The revenue supports the Ese'eja, the local Indian community. At the moment the lodge is still being run by Rainforest Expeditions, a Peruvian ecotourism company, but the Ese'eja staff are being trained to take it over. With all the logging and gold-mining in the area it was good to see money made from the forest in a less destructive way. People have sometimes asked me what they can do to help save the rainforests. My answer is this: go and visit them. Many of the remaining forests will only survive if they can bring in an income from tourism. Sadly, though, this is a fragile economy for local people: the Posada Amazonas lodge had been practically empty since the terrorist attacks of 11 September 2001.

It had been swelteringly hot all day, but that night a gentle breeze began to blow. 'It looks like rain tomorrow,' said Guillermo. We all felt relieved and, sure enough, the following day it did rain. But overnight the temperature had dropped dramatically — by about 10 degrees Celsius — and as we continued our boat journey, cold driving rain soaked us. It was a *Friaca*, a strange weather front that blows up from Patagonia. Mark had warned us about the heat, but he had said nothing about this. The Amazon is a place where you should expect the unexpected.

We didn't have many warm clothes to hand, but dug out whatever we could. My fleece was buried deep in the bottom of my case among our pile of luggage but Jake miraculously produced a soft cosy blanket. 'Don't know why I'm carrying this,' he said, 'but do you want to borrow it?'

'Oh, wow, — you're a star!' I said wrapping it round me. It had just won second prize after Rita's hairdryer for the most unexpectedly useful item to take on a tour of the Amazon jungle.

We spent the rest of the five-hour journey huddled together, shivering under a plastic sheet and were glad when at last we arrived at Tambopata — but the moment the boat had been moored at the jetty a wave of sandflies attacked. We grabbed our gear and hurried away from the river, cursing.

The base was set back a little way from the river. As we walked through the forest there were seeds that looked like sea urchins strewn across the path. Guillermo told me they were monkey-comb seeds, pointing up to a graceful smooth-limbed tree. As if to confirm it, a lanky shape swung into view, soft wispy back hair shining in the sunlight. It was a spider monkey, and another came to join it, hanging spread-eagled, its tail hooked round the branch like a third hand. I peered up at them with my binoculars, and saw that the first had a tiny baby clinging to her neck. The mother's black face was framed by shiny black hair that looked as though it had been combed forward, and the infant's huge eyes were agog, taking in the world.

Tambopata Research Centre was a simple thatched building standing on stilts in a small clearing. It was delightful, open to the forest, with hammocks slung on the veranda. We shared it with the small group of scientists who worked there, a couple of German birdwatchers and an English photographer. As we chatted in the evening, by candlelight, we revelled in the cosy atmosphere but we were all suffering badly with sandfly bites — Jake counted forty-five on one forearm alone. Rita and I had also picked up chiggers weeks before at Villa Carmen. Chiggers are small mites abundant in fields, pastures and other grassy areas. The larvae climb on board an unfortunate passer-by and insert their mouth parts, which causes horrible itching. It was worst at night and I lay awake, tossing and turning under the torn mosquito net. Every rustle and scratch could be heard through the bamboo partition walls. No doubt to the bemusement of neighbours, I had occasionally taken to slapping the bites to stop myself scratching them and creating sores that would get infected. Perhaps even worse than the chiggers was the thought of being bitten by the phlebotomine sandfly which carries a horrific disease called leishmaniasis, which is a parasitic infection that produces ulcers and lesions all over the body or eats away at the mucous membranes around the throat cavities producing grotesque disfigurement as though one's face has been eaten away. Guillermo told us that sores that won't heal can be an indication of leishmaniasis and we took to neurotically inspecting our bites and wounds at frequent intervals.

Before dawn the following day we headed back to the river. Today we were to travel to the base of a sheer cliff where the current sweeps round the outer edge of a bend, creating a vortex so powerful that the river rips into the bank, pulling down anything in its path, almost as though it had teeth. In some places rivers destroy up to 25 metres of forest every year, but here as the water had carved away at the steep bank it had created a cliff, revealing rare riches. Lying exposed are clay and mineral deposits and to some creatures this is the ultimate treasure.

The sky was still pale when a cacophony of raucous cries and squawks first carried across the water to us. Suddenly the air was full of birds — blue-headed parrots, mealy parrots and macaws, wheeling overhead before landing on the cliffs, fluttering about to find the best positions. The clay is high in salts and minerals, and it may be that the birds need the salts and minerals as a supplement to their diet of fruit and seeds, but perhaps there is more to it than that. Plants encourage animals to eat their fruit to disperse the seeds. However, as they certainly don't want the seeds themselves to be crunched up and consumed, so these are laced with poisons such as tannins and alkaloids. As the toxins build up in a seed-eater's system, they may prove fatal. But these birds had discovered that the clay neutralises the toxins and demand for it is so high that they have evolved a kind of rota system to collect it, with the smaller species arriving first and later the large macaws.

'Guacamayo', or 'he who calls on the river', is the local Quechua name for macaws, and by eight o'clock the noise was deafening when the garrulous scarlet, red-and-green, blue-and-yellow macaws began to appear in twos and threes. Their brilliant colours were reflected in the mirror-like surface of the river. They wheeled in in a spectacular aerial display, pairs flying in perfect formation, flashing their colours in unison: the yellow undersides of the blue-and-yellow macaws shone brazen against the pastel sky. As each pair prepared to land on the cliff, they banked in perfect synchrony, tilting their bodies simultaneously to flash the stunning bright blue of their backs.

We were there in September, at the end of the dry season, when clay-eating is at its peak. This may be because food supplies dwindle at this time of year, causing the macaws to fall back on poisonous toxic seeds and increasing the need for a detox. However, although eating the clay is important, it is also a social occasion for the birds. As photographer Frans Lanting put it, 'To assume that macaws go to the clay lick only to eat clay would be like saying that people only go to the pub because they are thirsty.' The birds sorted themselves into groups of different species so that the cliff was striped with bands of green, turquoise and red along the seams of minerals. There was a constant squawking as families arrived and left and others squabbled over bits of clay. The youngsters were spoilt — even though they were perfectly able to feed themselves, their parents frequently tore off lumps of clay to offer to them.

Between visits to the cliff face, many birds landed in a small grove of trees close to where we stood on a small island in the river, a little way back from the cliff. Away from the hubbub on the cliffs it was very much a 'couples party'. Often the pairs moved in unison, turning simultaneously to face the opposite way on a branch, each lifting a foot to claw the air or bowing together as though the choreography had been carefully rehearsed. On other branches, some regurgitated clay for their partners while others preened each other. Above us a scarlet macaw spun upside down on a branch, showing off to impress his mate. Then she followed suit. It was all delightfully flirtatious.

Until recently little was known about macaw

behaviour in the wild but that is changing, thanks to research at Tambopata and other sites. Macaws live for thirty to forty-five years in the wild, sixty to seventy in captivity, and among most species couples remain faithful to each other all their lives, their relationship repeatedly reaffirmed by the touching displays of affection we had witnessed. Compatibility between partners seems to be vital for breeding success, and parenting is not necessarily an inherited skill: often a first brood dies, and while a female usually lays two eggs, even in subsequent broods the second chick rarely survives. Chicks remain with their parents for about three years, but are fully grown by six months. Young birds can be distinguished by their eye colour: they have dark irises that turn paler with age.

All macaws have declined seriously in the wild, but the most critical situation faces the Spix macaw, whose wild population is almost certainly reduced to just one bird, identified as a male. There are thirty in captivity and attempts are being made to reintroduce captive birds to the wild to build up a population. Sadly, though, the last, wild Spix seems unaware of his importance and prefers to hang out with an Illiger's macaw.

The main cause of the macaw's demise is the destruction of their rainforest habitat, and the second is the pet trade. For every macaw that reaches a dealer, ten die in transit. Luckily export of macaws is now banned, but as their reproductive rate is low, it will be hard for their populations to recover.

One of the main reasons for macaw's inability to breed fast is that they won't attempt it without a suitable nest site. Early studies have suggested that out of a hundred pairs only between ten and twenty will try to reproduce in a given year, and six to fourteen fledglings will survive. Most macaws nest in tree cavities over thirty metres from the ground. Blue-and-yellow macaws favour the tops of dead palm trees; the scarlet and red-and-green species nest in hardwoods where a cavity has been created after a large branch has fallen. Because the Amazon is such a dynamic ecosystem old trees are in short supply, and in an area of a couple of square kilometres there may be just one or two suitable sites, which several pairs of birds will fight over.

The most important tree in this context is probably the mature Dipteryx, locally known as 'shihuahuaco'. It is wide-spreading, with fat limbs and neat, inviting round holes. Just one old tree can provide many nest holes, not just for macaws but for other animals and birds too. Unfortunately, the Peruvian government has recently encouraged the felling of Dipteryx for charcoal production. Large specimens are already rare and their removal could mean disaster for scarlet and red-and-green macaws. However, the research team at Tambopata have successfully pioneered the use of artificial nesting boxes.

Intelligent and gregarious, macaws are the primates of the bird world, and as pets they lavish the same affection on their owners as they would on a mate. But I much prefer to see them

112

socialising with their own kind and flying free.

We took several days over filming at the clay lick. One morning Si and I concealed ourselves in a small hide at the base of the cliff, among the swirling colour as the birds arrived. We had to be very quiet: macaws have traditionally been hunted at places like this, so they can be nervous. They are also vulnerable to wildcats and birds of prey.

As the morning progressed it became very hot in the heavy canvas hide. The air didn't pass through, but millions of sandflies did, biting our exposed wrists, necks and faces. Then there was a low rumble. Si and I peered out cautiously just as a mini landslide of small rocks and loose earth tumbled down the cliff face.

There was a grinding sound and more earth came down, a small boulder ricocheted off an outcrop and bounced past the hide. Above us, a large overhang looked unstable. I was glad when the macaws had finished their detox session and left the cliff so that we could escape.

The same forces that are undercutting these cliffs are having a different influence on the other side of the river. After we had left Tambopata, we headed to Manu National Park. Once again our journey was by boat, this time along the Manu river. I hadn't expected to come across beaches in the Amazon, but as the rivers erode one side they deposit the material they have carved away on the other, creating beautiful white stretches of sand covered in clouds of yellow and white butterflies. But these are a bit wilder than your average holiday beach.

On one pristine stretch a white-necked heron was hunched over, subduing a catfish, its long grey feathers ruffled like a scruffy old coat. A few feet behind it, a large black caiman basked in the sun. It eyed us as the current brought our canoe close alongside it. It was a formidable-looking animal, about 2.5 metres long, its tail jagged like the blade of a chainsaw. It opened its mouth to expose a row of lethal teeth, and then, quick as a flash, it moved forward and slipped into the deep brown water, disappearing under the surface in front of us.

The beaches are important breeding grounds for turtles and many birds. Plovers and terns nest there, and on one occasion I saw a pair of skimmers calling plaintively to each other as they swapped nest duty. In the early morning some beaches are covered in dozens of small, sandy-coloured night hawks, their feathers fluffed up while they sleep. On closer inspection you see that the beach is actually covered in tiny sandy-coloured chicks trusting to the camouflage of their feathers to keep them safe.

The beaches look like a haven of tranquillity, but in fact they are a war zone, where the jungle is fighting to claim back territory from the rivers. After checking for caimans we walked up a stretch of sand — treading carefully to avoid turtle eggs or hawk chicks. Near the forest edge we found a carpet of Tessauria seedlings, the first to invade the beach with airborne seeds. The river is at its weakest during the dry season and they must quickly entrench their position, sending down roots to take a firm hold or they will be washed away the next time the river floods. As the Tessaurias grow they become secure in the sandy soil and provide shade so that other plants can follow: first cane, then the fast-growing Cercropia, or balsawood trees. Each successive wave of plants creates conditions that enable the next to germinate and grow, until finally true rainforest is established once more.

As you make your way deeper into the forest, the rivers gradually lose momentum, meandering in ever more circuitous curves and loops. When there has been heavy rain, though, they tear a new path through the forest, severing the neck of a meander and leaving behind a crescent-shaped ox-bow lake. These sleepy backwaters are home to some of the Amazon's most rare and wonderful animals, and we were hoping to find them.

We tend to think of the rainforest as one vast homogeneous forest, but in fact it is a mosaic of different neighbourhoods that change constantly, creating a wealth of different opportunities for animals, which in turn leads to a huge variety of life. Manu National Park is the size of Switzerland and is one of the richest places on earth: nearly 3,500 different species of plant have been recorded, 200 mammal species and, in just four square kilometres, 530 bird species.

Just before sunset we arrived at Casa Machiguenga, a lodge built and run by the local Machiguenga people. As we approached, someone was lighting the little oil lamps that lined the paths leading to small huts roofed with palm fronds. The trees rustled around us and in the far distance we detected a wave of sound like a distant jet — the howler monkeys were roaring.

Moments later there was a piercing shriek from one of the huts. Rita had just opened a case, which was crawling with cockroaches. No sooner had we got rid of them than there was another yell — this time from the boys' hut. We found Si with a fantastic caterpillar some three centimetres long, with red dots, yellow feet and black and white branched spines. It had been on the railing, which he had gripped and the poisonous spines had penetrated his hand. He was in a lot of pain. Squashing a caterpillar might not seem like a big deal but in South American forests it can be dangerous. I had heard of a man who had crushed the caterpillar of the saturnid moth with his bare knee. He was admitted to hospital some days later, with severe headaches, fever and dark urine thick with blood. Later he became mentally confused and lost the power of speech. Despite a series of blood transfusions his condition deteriorated and sixteen days after contact with the caterpillar he lost consciousness. The doctors tried everything to save him — but four days later he died of a massive cerebral haemorrhage.

Mark hurried to fetch one of the Machiguenga Indians. He wore a long woven smock and his shiny, straight black hair was cut sharply at the shoulders and short across his brow. He had deep-set eyes, a high forehead and a solemn air as he looked at the caterpillar. He told us not to worry and bandaged Si's hand with a poultice of damp tobacco leaves. Tobacco originates in

South America and is important in local medicine, used topically to soothe bites, stings and rashes. In Si's case, it proved effective.

The next day we left before dawn for Cocah Salvador, an ox-bow lake isolated from the main river by a stretch of forest. There, we climbed into a small boat and paddled out on to the water, now suffused with the soft gold light of dawn. At first only the faint splashing of our paddles broke the silence as the canoe glided through the ethereal mist floating over the water. But within minutes the forest was waking up. The warbling notes of a pair of green ibis, the chiming melody of the black-faced ant thrush and the delicate double chime of the ant bird were joined by the gentle two-tone whistle of the sun bittern, the hesitant wolf-whistles of an undulated tinamou and the tuneful trills of dusky titi monkeys. Gradually more and more animals greeted the day and in amongst the pretty whistles, trills and churring came the loud honking of cormorants and a bizarre sound, like a two-stroke being started: the call of a piping guan.

As we paddled up the lake, a small green kingfisher dived into the water, a flock of white-winged swallows skimmed the surface, catching insects, while a small sun grebe with a reddish face, black cap and white stripe, swam along with a flotilla of ducks and ducklings leaving a sparkling V-shaped wake. Then, a hundred metres ahead, there was an abrupt splash. Swimming directly towards us, in formation, we saw three giant river otters, their heads held above the water. They were large but not quite 'giant', I thought. One dived under the water and surfaced beside the boat. I leaned over and found myself gazing into a wide brown face with large bright eyes and long whiskers dripping with water. It was a juvenile and, after investigating us briefly, it swam back to its companions and started to play around the branches of a dead tree in the water. Then we saw a fourth otter, a large female nearly two metres long resting on the log. Perhaps this was the breeding female. Only one pair in each family group of otters breeds, and during the two months that the cubs stay in the den everyone looks after them, but principally their older siblings. Unlike most otters, this species is highly sociable: they need each other as defence against their arch-enemy, the black caiman. They are fiercely protective of the young — by working as a team they've even been known to see off jaguars.

The breeding female is the dominant member of the group, leading the rest and initiating activities such as hunting. Adults can eat up to three kilos of fish each day; when the breeding female is lactating she consumes as much as five. In Spanish these otters are called *lobos del rio* or 'river wolves', because of the way they hunt: they swim under water in a phalanx to drive fish together, taking it in turns to come to the surface to breathe. Their whiskers are sensitive to any currents, which helps them detect the fishes' direction.

Sometimes, as we watched, the otters swam

The cinebulle, a motorised balloon, gave us a fantastic bird's eye view over the canopy.

Above: Dany expertly guides the cinebulle low over the branches while Si films aerials.

Left: The envelope acted like a giant sail, catching the wind and buffetting me around as I pulled my way up the rope 200 feet into the canopy.

The only way to really appreciate the dangers for animals living high in the Borneo trees is to climb them. Si hauls himself and the camera up the tree, dwarfed by the giants around him.

Below: Despite my fear of heights I felt safe perched 150 feet up in the arms of this giant mengarris, the tallest of all rainforest trees, and said to harbour the forest spirits.

Orang-utans spend most of their lives at heights of 180 feet in the canopy. Infants aren't born climbers, so orphaned orang-utans are taken to the forest by the carers from the sanctuary so they can learn how to get about as well as learn what foods to eat.

The night time population of the forest explodes as half a million wrinkle-lipped bats emerge from their caves in the cliff and descend on the forest to feed.

A three-horned rhinoceros beetle which we met ambling across a liana. Its enormous curving horns are used for sparring with other males.

I emerge from a hollow strangler fig tree to greet Si.

Below: I am dwarfed by this gigantic bird's nest fern, one of the many plants that live up in the branches creating amazing tree-top gardens.

Right: James steadies the rope while Si climbs up onto the sleeping platform.

Inset right: Si and I getting shipshape on the platform 100 feet up in the canopy which was my bed for three nights.

Gibbons are the fastest flightless animals in the canopy, swinging through the trees at speeds of 35 kilometres per hour. Gibbons also regularly walk upright along the tops of branches, their arms stretched out like a tightrope walker.

Riding the rapids. The fast flowing Pilcopata river runs through the foothills of the Andes carrying a precious cargo of nutrients and sediment to fertilise the Amazon forest.

The breath of the forest. At dawn moisture from the forest rises above the canopy and condenses in the cool air, part of the process by which forests make rain.

The beautiful riverboat *The Delfin* took us exploring up the Amazon river.

The river in spate can tear up giant trees like this sacred ceiba, leaving them strewn in the water like crashed space rockets.

Tucked away in the sleepy backwaters of the Amazon are giant river otters.

Mark Flowers, our producer and resident artist, with Bandito the macaw at Villa Carmen.

The hairy caterpillar that Si brushed against which caused intense pain and required treatment by local Machiguenga Indians.

A carachama fish. The water is so warm here that it doesn't contain much oxygen so these fish can breathe air and are fine out of water.

I contemplate a very pretty pink-toed tarantula.

Paddling along in a canoe I hope to get close to some pink dolphins but instead find myself close to a black caiman.

ur relief at the arrival of the float plane at Cocha El Dorado as short-lived as it promptly got stuck on the muddy bank.

I am mesmerised by the sunset over the Amazon river. As it was above so it was all around.

An infant western lowland gorilla. His mother was shot by poachers for the burgeoning trade in 'bushmeat'. By learning about the forest it is hoped he may one day be returned to the wild.

An adolescent western lowland gorilla.

Below: A silverback gorilla takes his family out into the bai to feed on water lilies, and other aquatic plants. It's like one giant salad bowl.

Above: Andrea's camp at Dzanga Bai was well set up and I took advantage of having a desk to write up my notes.

This Weaver bird made its nest right in the middle of Andrea's camp seemingly unperturbed by our comings and goings.

It was fantastic to come across this open oasis in the forest filled with elephants and other animals. If you approached downwind of the animals you could get quite close.

Rich mineral seams beneath the water are tapped. Elephants may need these as an antidote to toxins in leaves. A young calf learns the best places from its mother.

Jake, James and Si wading through warm elephant dung on the way to Dzanga bai.

You suddenly feel very small and flimsy when out in the open and faced with a large elephant who is preparing to charge.

Three Ba'aka ladies show me how to prepare the medicinal plants they have collected from the forest.

The Ba'aka are very easygoing. Even though we couldn't speak each others' language Ekáso and I became good friends.

The Ba'aka make temporary camps in the forest by weaving together saplings and covering the framework in leaves.

The Ba'aka village of Yandombe where we met Louis Sarno.

Travelling along overgrown waterways to Mbeli in a rather unstable canoe.

together in groups, but fishing must have been easy on Cocha Salvador: wherever they dived they surfaced almost every time with a mouthful of fish. It was hard to keep track of who was who, as they kept disappearing under the water to re-emerge somewhere else. I was watching out for the youngster who had come to see us earlier. All otters have their own individual markings of white patches on their fur, which makes them easy to identify, and he had a large white patch on the left side of his throat. When I saw him come up from his dive, he was without a fish. Perhaps he still had to perfect his hunting technique.

As the morning wore on the character of the lake changed. The birds stopped calling and the shrill, metallic sound of insects took over. Swarms of orange dragonflies buzzed lazily over the surface of the languid, olive-coloured water. Suddenly we saw three otter kits emerge from a den in a pile of dead branches on the bank. They must have been two or three months old. Escorted by a juvenile, they teetered along the tree-trunk to where the others were lounging in the sun. In another month or so they would start hunting for themselves, but for now their older brothers and sisters produced food as soon as they begged. Eventually the adolescents would leave to start families of their own.

Giant river otters are highly endangered. They were nearly hunted to extinction for their fur. As many as twenty thousand pelts were exported from Brazil in the 1960s and now there are probably no more than three thousand left in the wild, fewer than four hundred in Peru. Despite a ban on hunting in the 1970s, their numbers are not recovering: deforestation, depletion of fish populations through overfishing, and mercury pollution due to gold-panning and extraction are narrowing the otters' chances of survival. Cocha Salvador was a rare oasis for them.

We had seen how rivers shaped the forest and the lives of the animals that lived there. Now we were going to explore the Amazon river — a river so huge that it can actually swallow the forest to create a unique environment: the flooded forest.

6

The Flooded Forest

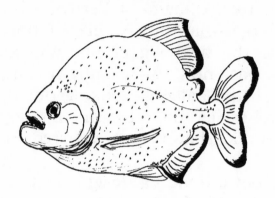

The building on the corner of the main square looked like a large metal box with a covered balcony running along two sides of the upper floor. 'It was designed by Gustave Eiffel,' said Mario, with the air of someone trying to sound more enthusiastic than he felt.

We were in Iquitos in north-eastern Peru, a town of decaying splendour. The largest rainforest city in the country, it had been at the centre of the lucrative rubber trade in the early twentieth century. The rubber barons' houses stand along the roads leading into the main square and, despite their peeling paint, are still magnificent, their grand façades covered with elegant Spanish tiles. Even the pavement had been painstakingly laid with them, but they were now worn, cracked and dirty. In its heyday Iquitos was immensely wealthy and, some said, even more glamorous than Paris.

It was still humming with life. At seven o'clock on a Thursday night, music and lights spilled out on to the streets, and pretty girls in short skirts strolled along the pavements. We had been rejoined by Roberto and had met up with Mario, our local fixer, Lilliana, a Peruvian doctor, and Paul, a larger-than-life American businessman, to discuss the next leg of our journey. Eiffel's building was now a restaurant and we sat upstairs on the balcony, looking out through its metal arches at the stream of mopeds and motorised rickshaws that whirred round the square.

'How does a building designed by Eiffel come to be in Iquitos?' I asked.

'It was originally built for a trade fair in Paris, where it was bought by a Bolivian rubber baron who had it flat-packed and shipped via North Africa across the Atlantic, then up the Amazon,' Paul explained. 'But it was accidentally put on a boat to Iquitos instead of to wherever it was meant to go in Bolivia, and it stayed as lost luggage until the baron died. His beneficiaries decided to sell it on locally so it was resurrected here.'

Iquitos' importance to the rubber trade stemmed from its location: it lies far into the forest on the uppermost reaches of the Amazon, which acts as a highway through the Amazon Basin. From here, traders had access, by water, to the large forest towns of Brazil, such as Manaus in central Amazonia, then all the way out to the Atlantic Ocean and beyond.

The scale of the Amazon river is mind-blowing — it's a natural for the *Guinness Book of Records*. It is 60,516 kilometres long, and that's not including the bends. At its uppermost reaches it is about two kilometres wide; around 1500 kilometres before it reaches the sea, it has expanded to 10 kilometres, and at its mouth it is a vast 320 kilometres, spilling 200 million litres every second into the Atlantic. It has 1100 tributaries, carries a fifth of all the river water in the world, contains more species of fish than the entire Atlantic and drains nearly half of South America. And every year, without fail, it bursts its banks, flooding at least 150,000 of the 5-6 million square kilometres of rainforest — an area the size of England or Iowa. It is the home of the largest flood in the world.

For half of the year this flooded forest, is much like any other, but for the other half its character changes dramatically. Each year six metres of rain from the cloud forest combine with meltwater from the snow-capped Andes, leading to a massive rush of water into the Amazon Basin. The Amazon itself, its mighty tributary the Rio Negro and many of the region's other vast rivers overflow. Because of their size it can take two months for the effects of the rain and snowmelt to become apparent, but when they do the impact is stupendous. The water penetrates 10-15 kilometres on either side of the main river channels, and in some places as far as 75 kilometres. It is anything from five to 16 metres deep.

Far from being a disaster, this flood creates

one of the most extraordinary places on earth: a topsy-turvy world in which trees become islands in an inland sea, piranhas swim where flowers once grew and eels hunt high among the branches of trees. Fish eat fruit and disperse the seeds of trees, some of which even germinate under water. The strange rooster-like hoatzin learns to swim before it can fly (even when it does fly it is clumsy and cumbersome) and builds its nest over water, providing a ready means of escape for chicks under threat from marauding capuchin monkeys.

When the water recedes there are other surprises such as fish that live out of water. In one of the black water tributaries of the Rio Negro there lives a very unusual creature called *Phreatobius walkeri* that is about four centimetres long and looks rather like a red worm. Recently scientists have decided that this bizarre creature is in fact a fish. During the flooded season it lives underwater in submerged leaf-litter but when the waters recede it can survive on the forest floor in a film of water by moving around amongst the moist leaf litter. Its vivid colour is due to high concentrations of haemoglobin in its blood which allows it to survive with very low levels of oxygen.

It is during the dry season that you can best explore the flooded forest and get close to some of its strange inhabitants. When the water is high the animals are spread thinly throughout the forest, but when it recedes many are concentrated in the rivers, streams and isolated pools. One such refuge is Cocha El Dorado, 'the golden lake', which lies beyond the upper reaches of the Amazon river. And that was where we were heading, in the hope of finding and filming pink dolphins.

The plan was to fly into El Dorado on a hydroplane, stay at a cabin owned by Mario, do our filming, then walk out of the jungle to the nearest navigable river. Here, we would be met by a boat that would take us to the Amazon itself, then change to a larger boat owned by Paul, which would bring us back to Iquitos.

Until now our journey through Peru had gone with Swiss-style precision, but things were about to change. The Peruvian air force, which owned the hydroplane we had booked, informed us that it was defunct. However, a smaller one was available and could fly us and our gear to El Dorado in two shifts. We agreed that Si and Jake would take the gear on the first flight and the rest of us would follow on the second.

Accordingly, at six the next morning, Si and Jake set off for the base. The rest of us had a slightly later start and went into town to buy supplies for the trip. We loaded up with essentials — endless cans of insect repellent, mosquito coils, loo paper, candles and three bottles of Colombian rum. Mario looked at these and raised his eyebrows. 'You want to see double the number of birds and caimans and dolphins, eh?'

The truth was that Rita had developed a talent for making pisco sour, a delicious drink made with rum, egg white and lemon juice. We didn't have the last two ingredients, but she was prepared to improvise. Anyway, we were going to be far from civilization for some time and there were bound to be thirsty times ahead.

Back at the hotel we learnt that the others had got half-way to El Dorado and had had to turn back due to bad weather and engine trouble. What was more, they were now stuck at the air-force base, some twenty minutes' drive out of town, because a small-scale war had erupted on the outskirts of Iquitos. We found out later that a suburb was being cleared of illegal squatters — around a hundred families had built houses on land they didn't own and were now being evicted. Si and Jake made it back to the hotel by early afternoon, relieved to be in one piece, and filled us in on the rest of the story.

'Once we got back to the base we sat around for hours. We eventually managed to get a boat upriver to bypass the trouble, walked back to the road, picked up a motor taxi for a short distance, then found another vehicle that could bring us into town. Not counting a donkey and a bicycle, we've been in almost every form of transport this morning and got absolutely nowhere,' Jake said.

Roberto laughed. 'Ah! Now you're seeing a bit of the real Peru.'

There was nothing else we could do, so we sat in the hotel lobby waiting for news. We had checked out of our rooms and were still hoping that we might be able to leave Iquitos that day. Someone pointed out that it was Friday the thirteenth. Our precious time was ticking away. While Mark was trying to come up with an alternative plan, Paul appeared and said we could use his boat, but we had already paid the air force for the hydroplane so we were keen to use it. From time to time Mark, Rita or Roberto would disappear to telephone the air force to find out if the engine had been fixed. Every time the answer was the same. They'd know whether the problem was serious in about half an hour. And so it went on.

Late in the afternoon we heard that the fighting had calmed down, so we went to the air-force base to find out at first hand what was happening and to pick up the gear that Si and Jake had been forced to abandon earlier. It turned out to be a few buildings on the edge of the river, and a rickety-looking hydroplane was surrounded by uniformed airmen in mirror shades, looking as if they'd walked straight out of *Top Gun*. The cowling behind one of the propellers was open and the engine exposed. I wished I hadn't seen it: it would have been more at home in a lawn mower than in a plane that was supposed to carry 300-400 kilos of equipment and several people. There was no evidence that any mechanical work was in progress. However, the *Top Gun* crowd thought that the plane would be ready to fly first thing in the morning, but told us we should confirm this with the commander.

In the event that the plane wasn't ready we had planned to take up Paul on his offer and leave that night, but it was now six thirty and we settled by the phone in the lobby while Rita and Roberto set out to find the commander. Most of the time Rita has the spirit of a playful girl, but if the need arises she can be firm. When the commander apologised and informed her that the engineer was not around and the plane would not be fixed for a few days, she said sternly, 'Sorry is just not good enough.'

Afterwards Roberto told us that he'd been a bit apprehensive about how the top brass in the Peruvian air force would react to being addressed like that, but apparently the commander had been sheepish and promised that if we could get out to El Dorado by some other means, a plane, possibly even the big one, would pick us up.

By now it was too late to leave anyway, so having spent at least 12 hours of the day in the lobby we decided to check back in to the hotel.

Early next morning we were introduced to Paul's boat. Appropriately, as we were going searching for dolphins, she was called the *Delfín*, and she was magnificent — a romantic old riverboat painted green and white, the perfect way to journey up the Amazon. We chugged up the wide expanse of coffee-brown water. At first the distant banks — about a kilometre away — were dotted with houses and cultivated with coffee and bananas, but gradually these gave way to wilderness. It was dazzlingly bright on the river after so long in the forest and on smaller waterways and wonderful to see such a big sky. As Mark and I pored over maps we felt a sense of awe and excitement.

Later we watched the sunset from the top deck — bold, glowing orange brushstrokes across an eggshell blue sky, and to the south-west bruised purple clouds and pink fluffy ones — one shaped like a wolf's head — piled up high on the horizon, edged with golden light. Cormorants flew over us in a perfect V formation on their way to roost, and a flock of snowy egrets passed low over the water, their legs outstretched behind them and their feathers tinged pink with the last rays. And as it was above, so it was all around us — enriched and reflected back in a vast liquid mirror. It's hard to describe the beauty of the place or the elation we felt that night, but as the gibbous moon rose we paid tribute to Pacha Mama and danced on the top deck while the slick dark waters of the Amazon parted along the bows of the *Delfín*.

Nothing about the Amazon is average. The following day we passed a side channel where I saw giant waterlilies the size of children's paddling-pools. These were *Victoria amazonica*, named in 1837 for the new young Queen by the distinguished plant collector John Lindley. Their geodesic pattern is said to have inspired Joseph Paxton's design of the Crystal Palace for the 1851 Great Exhibition in London. The giant Amazon waterlily is amazing not only in appearance but in its behaviour. The large white female flower, with a sweet butterscotch-like fragrance, attracts a scarab beetle carrying pollen. As the beetle enters, it brushes the pollen on to the stigma, fertilising the flower. But then the flower closes, trapping the hapless beetle and keeping it overnight as a reluctant guest while it works a little magic and transforms itself into a pink male flower. Peppered with pollen, the beetle is now allowed to leave and search out another sweet-smelling female flower — and the process begins again.

The river had stayed a relatively constant width of about two kilometres, but now it was widening. A little further upstream it opened out into a vast sea stretching away in all directions. It took us a moment to realise that we had come to the head of the Amazon, to the place where it is born from the merging of two other huge rivers, the Ucayali and the Marañón. We spent a long time filming there, making forays up the different rivers and circling on the vast empty expanse of water where they met, before continuing up the left fork, the Ucayali. It was time to say goodbye to the *Delfín*. We saluted its captain and crew and transferred to a smaller boat to take us the rest of the way to Requina, the last town before the jungle.

We arrived after dark, and decided to leave non-essential gear in the boat as transport wasn't easy. We loaded the rest on to four motorised rickshaws and headed off into the night, bumping along a dirt track torn up by deep erosion gullies. Five minutes from the port we entered a ramshackle town where the road changed to a patchwork of tarmac and potholes, and drew up in front of the Hotel Plaza, a rundown establishment that didn't in any way deserve its grand-sounding name. In the middle of the small lobby a torn plastic sofa faced a television with Julie Andrews as Mary Poppins singing 'Let's Go Fly A Kite' in Spanish. A girl gestured along the corridor towards rooms at the back. The windows were broken and the sheets grubby, but the rickety fans worked (despite the bare wires hanging out of them) and we were too exhausted to be fussy. But before we could collapse into bed we had to discuss the plan for phase two of our journey, which would take us to Cocha El Dorado.

We sat at a table on the pavement under a fluorescent strip-light buzzing with insect life and ate a rudimentary meal while everyone talked at once. Ever since the hydroplanes had failed us, our strategy had become rather *ad lib*, but from now on, with no shelter or food available until we got to Mario's place at El Dorado, we needed a firm plan.

'How long will it take us to get across to the Yanayacu?' Mark asked. The Yanayacu river fed into Cocha El Dorado, and between it and where we were on the Ucayali there was a stretch of forest we would have to cross on foot.

'Maybe one day,' said Victor, a colleague of Mario's who had joined us to assist with this part of the journey.

'No,' scoffed Mario, 'about five hours.' Then he added, a little haughtily, 'Depending on how fast you walk.'

'How long is the canoe journey on the other side?' someone else asked.

Again, there was a difference of opinion between our fixers. Mark looked worried — he was responsible for getting his crew and all of the equipment safely to and from El Dorado and needed definite answers — but the rest of us were secretly hoping for adventure. Victor and Mario eventually came to some kind of consensus, and Victor wrote out the schedule on a napkin.

When we set off the herringbone sky was just tinged with pink. The harbour was full of long wooden boats piled high with bananas and vegetables and as the sky became a deeper pink and gold we watched vultures arrive to scavenge in the glistening mud for rotting vegetable matter. It was a scene of picturesque squalor. We stopped briefly in a small fishing village to hire some porters to help us with our gear, and then we were dropped off on a wide sandy bank. In the distance a small path led into the forest.

It was exceptionally hot and a relief to get out of the sun, away from the glare of the water. Tall, straight-limbed trees emerged from a thick undergrowth of bushes and tangled vines. It looked like a normal stretch of forest until Roberto pointed out a water-mark on a tree about four metres up. It was strange to think that for up to six months of the year this whole area was under water.

Many of the trees that occur in the flooded forest are the same species as those found in the parts of the Amazon that don't experience flooding — the so-called *terra firme* forest — or are closely related to them: for example, there are two similar species of Astrocaryum palm, one of which is widespread in flooded forests while the other is found only in *terra firme*. But some of the trees we saw are unique to the flooded forest: castanharanas, which are related to the brazil-nut tree; wild soursop, whose domesticated cousin produces the delicious custard-apple and the piranha-tree (named not after the fish but after a noctuid moth that pollinates it). Along the riverbanks where full sunlight beams down, vines such as those of the gourd family *Cucurbitacae* are prolific.

Most plants would die from lack of oxygen if their roots remained waterlogged for any length of time, yet trees in the flooded forest are somehow designed to cope with long periods of inundation. No one is really sure how they have adapted to do this: the most obvious solution to the problem is aerial roots that remain above the flood-line, but only a very small number of flooded forest species have adopted this ploy. The rest must have another, more efficient system that we haven't worked out yet.

The plants of the understorey spend much of their infancy under water, having grabbed whatever sunlight they can during the low-water season in order to photosynthesise and grow. While forest trees are submerged, they retain their leaves and some photosynthesis takes place under water.

I spotted a burrow the size of a rabbit hole at the base of a tree: it probably belonged to a tarantula. Terrestrial animals would drown if they remained on the forest floor all year round, so they tune in to several environmental signs, such as increasingly waterlogged soil and raised humidity, that warn of the approaching floods. Then spiders, millipedes, centipedes, beetles, terrestrial molluscs and segmented worms — all of which normally lurk in the leaf litter — scurry up the tree-trunks to escape the rising waters. Once in the canopy, they hide under loose pieces of bark or among the leaves of bromeliads and other epiphytic plants. But the floodwaters are not the only danger: spiders and lizards form an advance guard in the huge exodus, taking up prime positions higher on the trees so that when other species follow they are perfectly situated to make the most of this upwardly mobile feast.

Ants are the most common insect in the flooded forest and consequently there are many examples of 'ant plants'. Cecropia trees grow here and when the forest floods, the colony of resident Azteca ants move upwards, becoming increasingly marooned on the umbrella-shaped crown of their hosts.

As we trudged on, a noisy troop of squirrel monkeys leapt along the branches overhead. Animals that can fly or climb above the water-mark have no need to move out when the waters rise, so the canopy is full of monkeys. I kept a keen look-out for the black uakari, the local species of a bizarre bald monkey. Its cousin has a bright red face which makes it look badly sunburnt and has given rise to the local name, *macaco inglés*, or 'English monkey'. Uakaris are found only in the flooded forest. They are very active in the canopy, moving in large, loose groups of thirty to fifty individuals (sometimes up to a hundred), travelling considerable distances and rarely coming to the ground. They feed on the abundant fruit that ripens during flood times, as well as leaves, nectar, the seeds of immature fruits and some insects, especially caterpillars. Severely endangered, they are hunted for food in Peru and for bait in Brazil, where people won't eat them because of their human-looking faces.

On the other side of this strip of land we were to pick up the canoes that would take us up the Yanayacu river to Cocha El Dorado. As they belonged to the local fishermen we had expected small dugouts, but instead there was quite a range of canoes of different sizes, including a large one with a small outboard motor that could take all of us and most of the gear. It seemed the obvious choice — but in retrospect was a big mistake.

Once we were under way, we entered one of the most beautiful places I've ever seen — a watery grassland, which was a haven for birds. Sandpipers and wattled jacanas marched along little sandbanks; bright yellow-headed orioles landed on branches over the river; and families of macaws flew overhead, glowing turquoise and gold against the lapis sky. A tiger heron waded about in the water in front of us, lazily stretching out wide wings and taking off as we approached. Tall, elegant wood storks perched at the tops of trees along the banks. Every now and again a large ringed kingfisher dived in front of the canoe. We passed a black-collared hawk, a reddish brown bird the size of a buzzard, with a black ring like a bow-tie round its neck. It eyed us imperiously from its high vantagepoint.

It wasn't the only creature watching us carefully. The water was infested with caimans, mostly small ones but there were some big ones lying dead still in the shadowy vegetation overhanging the bank. One slipped into the water as we passed, a monster some four metres long. Black caimans are fearsome predators, active mostly at night and endowed with acute sight and hearing. They feed on fish such as piranha and catfish, and aquatic animals such as the capybara and the giant river otter. They've also been known to attack humans.

We made slow progress. The atmosphere felt close and sleepy, the low hum of our little engine a monotonous lullaby in the afternoon heat. The channel was getting narrower: we brushed under low-hanging branches and the aerial roots of fig trees, which looked like long dreadlocks tinged with henna. Then the boat engine sputtered and we came to a standstill. The driver revved the engine and it roared, but we didn't move. We were stuck, and there was nothing for it but to get out and push.

The water was warm, like bath water, but dark brown and murky — I was wearing *tevas*, which are open sandals, but the mud between my toes was repugnant. Then something brushed past my ankle. 'Agh! What was that?'

Si laughed and told me it was just a branch, but a moment later Roberto and Rita also exclaimed. The water was teeming with life — and the fish round there include piranhas — anacondas, stingrays and electric eels too. And, of course, we had watched the beady-eyed caimans slipping silently into the river. I noticed some greater yellow-headed vultures circling on the thermals high overhead. It was not a comforting sight.

About twenty metres upstream the channel became a little deeper and we got back into the boat, but not for long. Around the next bend a sandbank forced us to get out and push again. The sun was beating down and things grew more surreal by the minute. We passed a pool where a black caiman lay, watching us through thin, vertical pupils in its yellow, unblinking eyes. Suddenly, bubbles appeared all around us in the water as if it was gently shimmering. Ramón, a spry old man who had grown up in this strange world, reached into the water and came up with a fish. I was astounded and he laughed, stretched down and pulled out another. '*Es una carachama*,' he said proudly, as he held out an armour-plated catfish. It was a fantastic-looking creature, 30 centimetres long with a speckled belly and a greenish tortoiseshell pattern on the solid armour plating across its back. Ramón handed it to me and I ran my finger gingerly along its spiky dorsal fin — it was razor sharp. Another reason to tread carefully on the muddy bottom.

This is a world where, for six months of the year, fish rule. Nowhere else on earth do they swim through the branches of trees. The flooded forest provides a nursery for their young, plenty of places to hide and as much food as they can eat. The rising of the floodwaters triggers many of the trees to bear fruit, providing the fish with a veritable bonanza. Of the 2400-plus fish species in the Amazon, around 200 eat fruit and seeds

— that's many more than in tropical Africa or Asia. The large size of many of the fish enables them to carry more seeds than a bird or monkey could: a 15–30-kilo catfish can carry more than sixty large palm seeds, weighing more than two kilos in its stomach and intestines. Also, being able to swim freely from tree to tree helps with both feeding and seed dispersal.

There are other fish known to eat fleshy fruits such as soursop and figs. By covering its seeds in a fleshy layer the tree makes them more attractive as food — pulpy fruit appeals to animals that might not otherwise eat seeds — and also helps as a flotation device, enabling the seeds to travel further from the parent tree thus increasing dispersal prospects.

Fish seed-eaters include the infamous piranha and the oscar — favoured by the aquarium trade because of its attractive blue-black colouring, pale yellow markings and striking black and orange eye-spots — but perhaps the most important of all is the tambaqui. This enormous member of the characin family weighs up to 30 kilos and cruises through the waters of the forest looking for its favourite fruit trees, Spruce's rubber tree. This produces the largest seed of all the rubber trees and relies on the tambaqui for their dispersal. As the floodwaters rise the fruit matures and splits open, showering seeds into the surrounding water, where they float. The tambaquis' excellent sense of smell lures them to the fruiting trees and they gather underneath, waiting for this bounty to fall into the water around them.

When the water recedes the fish are left in ever-dwindling streams of warm, soupy water, which is also low in oxygen, because the solubility of oxygen in water decreases with a rise in temperature. Because of this the fish have adapted to their expanding and contracting world by learning to breathe air. This explains why Ramón's carachama had seemed more or less happy out of the water. The bubbling we had noticed earlier was fish coming to the surface to take huge gulps of air.

We were still marvelling at the carachama when another fish leapt out of the water and landed almost in Rita's lap. It was 60 centimetres long with big, mirror-like scales tinged with red. We stared at it in disbelief. It was an arawana, a cousin of the great paiche, or pirarucu, which is a voracious predator of other fish species, with teeth in its jaws *and* on its tongue. Also known as the redfish, the paiche is one of the largest freshwater fish in the world, reaching up to 3 metres in length and weighing 150 kilos.

The arawana can't compete with its vast relative, but still grows to a little over a metre. It is probably the largest fish in the world to specialise in eating insects, particularly beetles and spiders, but will also try to take small birds and bats — it has been reported that an arawana took two baby sloths. It has an amazing hunting strategy, which earns it its alternative name of 'water monkey': it can jump two metres out of the water, coiling its body and releasing it like a spring to propel it upwards to snatch insects from branches overhanging the water. Its large eyes also give it an advantage over other insect-eating fish: they have a split retina so that as the fish swims with the top part of its eye above water and the bottom half below it can see in both media at once. Thus it can spot insects falling from branches before they hit the water.

It was wonderful to study an arawana so closely, but we didn't want to keep it out of the water for too long and soon tossed it back. Mark was beside himself with excitement. 'In Japan the arawana is regarded as a very special fish — a symbol of life,' he told us.

'I'll never be able to eat another,' Roberto said, then added philosophically, 'But then again, death is part of life,' and the conversation turned to seviche, a delicious spicy dish made with lemon and raw fish.

As we continued upriver, we had to get out and push increasingly frequently. On one occasion we had physically to lift the canoe out of the water and drag it, with the gear on board, over a fallen tree that was blocking our way. All of this was playing havoc with Victor's napkin schedule. The journey had taken us far longer than we expected and it was getting late. It was disquieting to wade through caiman-infested waters in daylight — but it would be considerably worse at night.

At last we entered a broad waterway and up ahead was a wide lake, painted with the golden light of sunset, living up to its name of El Dorado. On the far side there were twin floating islands of grass and strange palms that looked like something out of Dr Doolittle. Now, during the dry season, they were anchored, but as the waters rose they would set sail together and float about on the lake.

Mario's place was called Refugio and consisted of a small wooden building set back 20 metres from the lake. It was built on stilts with steps running down the front. 'When the floodwaters rise you can take the canoe right up to the steps,' he told us. It had a small, covered veranda, and the rest was divided by half-partition walls into four tiny rooms. A plastic table and chairs were squeezed into one, and off it there were two shoeboxes with two bunkbeds apiece, and a kitchen. With the two Indian women who were going to cook for us, an Italian girl who had been recruited to prepare the place for tourism, and our boatman, a dozen of us were to share this home. It wasn't easy to see how we would all fit into it.

It was dark when I went down to the lake for a wash. I was alert for caimans, but Mario had also warned me not to swim too far out into the lake as there were piranhas. I tried not to think about the life that lurked in the inky water as I sploshed about in the shallows. Then something bit me. I leapt out of the water and nearly out of my skin. With my torch I examined the wound. It hadn't drawn blood — a hungry fish, perhaps, but not a piranha.

While the piranha's ferocious reputation is exaggerated — some are harmless herbivores, feeding on seeds and aquatic plants — four of the twenty-something species are thought to be dangerous to humans, particularly during the

141

low-water season when there is little food around. Some literally strip the flesh off their prey with their sharp, triangular teeth. The young of the red-bellied piranha start life feeding on insects and small crustaceans, progressing with adulthood to birds, rodents, other mammals, reptiles and frogs. In fact, they will feast on pretty much anything that falls into the water, from chicks to sloths. Several days later I witnessed an impressive demonstration of the damage piranhas can do when I was filmed putting some pieces of fish on a line and throwing it overboard. Within moments it was being savagely ripped apart by hordes of fish, and more kept coming. With our pole camera we were able to monitor the action under the surface and it wasn't pretty.

Our main mission at Cocha El Dorado, though, was to look for *botos*, or pink river dolphins. These are as elusive as they are strange. They were around — occasionally we'd catch a tantalising glimpse as the surface of the water spilled off shiny wet skin that was, indeed, distinctly pink, or we heard a belching sound, but that was it.

Apparently botos are attracted by noise — they are inquisitive creatures. Mario lent me his whistle and encouraged me to slap the water and bang the side of the boat, none of which made any difference. We decided to go a step further and returned to the cabin to collect a minidisc-player, speakers and an eclectic selection of music. I wasn't sure what the dolphins' taste might be, so I tried some banging techno, then some trancy stuff favoured by Roberto, followed by Ella Fitzgerald, a touch of Chopin, a little Miles Davis and so on. But if the dolphins were enjoying my top DJ mix, they didn't show it. They were milling about some distance away, fishing busily. Perhaps it was up to me to go over to them and introduce myself.

I climbed into a small, unstable dugout and paddled across. The dolphins obviously preferred this to the large boat and I could see them swimming beneath me. But as far as the cameras were concerned it was still a game of hide and seek. All we ever saw were tantalizing glimpses.

'Behind you!' Mark said, through the walkie-talkie in my pocket, and I whisked round just in time to see the water close — yet again — over a sleek pink back.

These dolphins are the stuff of legend, believed by local people to have exceptional powers. They are rarely hunted, but it is said that if a man adorns his wrist with the ear of a dolphin his virility increases dramatically. If a woman becomes pregnant and the father is not known the dolphins are blamed: like sirens, they are supposed to lure away women for secret liaisons at night.

Botos look quite different from other dolphins, with a long, slender snout, bulbous head and small dorsal fin. At about two metres long they are much the same size as some marine dolphins but are the world's largest fresh-water species. They are nearly blind, but in this murky freshwater world good eyesight would not be much use anyway. Instead, they rely largely on

143

echolocation to get around.

Echolocation is the reason for the bulbous 'melon' on top of the boto's head. Muscular movement forces air through special sacs inside it. The sounds produced travel through the water and when they encounter an object they are bounced back and received by the 'melon' and also by receptors on the boto's jaw mandibles. Unlike marine dolphins, botos have a flexible neck, which allows them to move their head from side to side in a sweeping motion, thus scanning a wider area in a single sweep without having to move their body. This is particularly useful in their cluttered freshwater environment where numerous objects in the water might otherwise obstruct navigation.

I liked paddling around the lake in the canoe even though it was highly unstable and kept filling with water. But I was also aware that the water was probably teeming with piranhas, caimans and the odd anaconda. I paddled up an inlet and there indeed, floating in the water, was a massive black caiman, its eyes visible above the surface. It was about the same length as the canoe and moving upstream very slowly. I overtook it and headed round the corner from where I was to paddle back to the main boat while delivering a piece to camera about El Dorado. The caiman followed me and I kept a close eye on it. Then suddenly it submerged, vanishing into the dark water. My heart pounded. Where was it? Was it going to flip the canoe over? I let out a cry as an almighty splash sounded directly behind me. I spun round in my seat, paddle raised above my head, ready to fend off my attacker. But it must have been only an enormous paiche, which had leapt in the water. The caiman was nowhere to be seen.

Back on the main boat the others had heard the splash and my exclamation. Mark and Rita called, 'Charlotte, are you okay?'

Jake was listening through his headphones. Ever the comedian, he muttered, 'Oh, no, it's got her. I'm picking up a loud, crunching sound on her mike.'

A moment later I appeared round the corner unscathed, delivering my piece but paddling slightly faster than usual. 'That caiman gave me a fright — it was huge!' I said, as I came alongside the big boat.

'You big wuss — it was a baby,' said Si. 'Now, off you go — do it again and this time try not to look like you're trying to break the water-speed record.'

After ten days of this, I felt as if we had been at El Dorado a lifetime. The lake was beautiful and we spent our days watching and filming the wildlife. But the nights were becoming increasingly difficult: we were low on food, except, of course, fish. (We were shocked to find that the fish on our plates most nights was oscar: intelligent fish that make prized pets in Europe, the US and Japan). The mosquitoes were the most vicious I've ever come across, descending in droves as soon as the sun went down to suck us dry. Even covered with our most potent, triple X-rated carcinogenic insect repellent we could not spend more than a few minutes at a time outside after dark without being eaten alive. Consequently we were all cramped into the tiny stuffy room around the plastic table, flicking out of our cups the little black bugs that fell off the overhead fluorescent light. Marialena, one of the cooks, put lurid green liquid on Rita's and my bites to soothe the itching, thereby turning us into a fair imitation of green-spotted Dalmatians. Sleeping was equally torturous: there was always a choir of snoring and the slightest movement, such as someone turning over in bed, made the whole cabin creak and groan.

Mario and the local Indians had set up a co-operative and were hoping to bring in visitors and some additional revenue. Given the remote location, they were never going to attract mass tourism, but I decided that they would have to rethink the accommodation or risk pathological behaviour among their guests. Cabin fever was getting to us and we began to look forward to the day when the hydroplane would pick us up. Would the commander keep his promise to Rita? We had a satellite phone, but it was temperamental and we hadn't been able to talk to him for some days.

On the appointed day we were on the lake trying for the last time to get some shots of the botos when we heard a plane. We whooped with joy as it came into view. It was the hydroplane — and, what was more, it was the big one: we could all leave together. We packed up the camera and sound gear, and headed across the lake as it came into land, jets of water spraying out from under its landing skis.

The Peruvian air force were looking as cool as ever in their dark blue uniforms and mirror shades. There were enthusiastic greetings and handshakes all round as we loaded up the plane and hopped in. The engines kicked into life, but the plane stood rooted in the mud at the edge of the lake. Several people on the shore leant their weight against the nose, but it wouldn't budge. Roberto and Si disembarked to help push and we all made to follow.

'Would the women please remain on board,' said the commander, looking at Rita and me, so we demurely sat down again, feeling slightly stupid. Moments later we were pleased we had. The boat had been brought over to tow the plane off the mud. It had only a five-horsepower engine, and instead of tying the line to the boat then driving off, several people on board held it as the boat attempted to reverse. We were laughing as the line went taut and threatened to pull everyone overboard, but at that moment, engines revving, the plane came free, and spun round, with the rotor-blade whirring across the boat's prow at head height.

'Duck!' someone shouted, and thankfully everyone did, just in the nick of time.

Now the plane was free, but we discovered that only one engine was working. To keep it afloat and stop it spinning in circles the pilot kept the revs up, ruddering it from side to side to keep it under control. Somehow all the lads were going to have to get from the boat on to the wildly careering plane. It was like a scene from *Apocalyse Now*. The boatman looked terrified as he tried to get alongside the plane while the commander shouted orders at the pilot. Eventually the boat was within a couple of metres of the plane. If the lads were going to board it was now or never.

'Go, go, *go!*' shouted the commander, as he urged each man off in quick succession. They leapt from the boat on to the float ski and hauled themselves inside the cabin. Last aboard was the commander: he jumped on just as the plane lurched away from the boat.

Minutes later we were racing across the surface of the lake and then we were airborne, on our way back to Iquitos. Dolphin and caimans were temporarily forgotten as we dreamt of hot showers and cold beers.

7

The Underworld

It was one o'clock in the morning and we were standing in the lobby of a dismal hotel in Libreville, Gabon, in West Africa. Our flight from Yaounde in Cameroon via Douala had had us hanging around in hot, sweaty and mostly deserted airports for the better part of the last twenty-four hours with nothing to do but play practical jokes on each other. More than once I'd had to remove a sticky baggage label saying 'In Transit to Congo' from my back.

Now, having failed to persuade the sleepy receptionist to get us a snack, we were trying to talk him into finding us some bottled drinking water. We were tired and hungry — but we were getting close to our goal. The following morning we would be away from cities: we had chartered a small plane to take us from Libreville to northern Congo and into the heart of the rainforest. Gaston, the representative of the charter company, had asked us to be at the airport at eight o'clock sharp. Our plane wasn't scheduled to leave until about ten, but he'd taken one look at our forty-eight cases of equipment and realised that if the police and Customs decided to be awkward we could be there for hours.

We arrived at the airport as instructed and met up with Boo Maisels, a stalwart Englishwoman, who was the research co-ordinator at Bomassa Research Centre, where we were headed, and was going to act as our guide. Gaston seemed unsure where our plane was but asked us to unload the gear at the Aero Club, where there were ranks of two-, four- and six-seater Cessnas and Pilatus Porters — many of which looked decidedly unairworthy. Ours was apparently a 'six-seater Pilatus Porter with a Y in its registration'. As I scanned the planes I was quite relieved that I couldn't see it.

Eventually Gaston discovered that ours was parked at the other end of the airport. By then we had lost one of our minibuses, so an obliging taxi driver rammed his cab full of cases, tent bags and the tripod, and set off after the remaining minibus, his suspension groaning and exhaust backfiring.

We wandered past a hangar where a forlorn Air Gabon plane stood waiting to be resurrected, then an Air France jumbo boarding passengers in their crisp travelling clothes, and found our Pilatus Porter. The pilot, a young South African called Richard, was leaning against the wing with his head in his hands. It wasn't a good sign. 'I have a problem with the wing flaps. I think I can fix it, but I'm waiting for a call from the mechanic to take me through it,' he said, then turned round — looking surprisingly cheerful in the circumstances.

Gaston told us to go back and wait at the Aero Club. Things weren't looking great: even if the plane was fixed it would not be able to take all of us and the kit.

An hour later we heard that Richard had failed to fix his wing flaps but that another plane was available. It was waiting for us on the other side of the airport. We loaded up the bags into an even more rickety taxi. The new plane was bigger and looked as if it could take us all in one run. The pilot, however, was quick to burst our bubble of optimism. His name was Johann and he balked at taking five passengers and 650 kilos of baggage in one load. After much standing around, hot and bad-tempered, on the tarmac it was decided that Nigel, the director of this shoot, Si, Jake and I would go on the first run with the immediately essential kit, while James, who was with us again to rig trees, would come with the rest as soon as another flight could be arranged. But no one was going anywhere just yet. We sat and waited for another five hours.

By three p.m. we were decidedly twitchy. We had to arrive at Kabo airstrip before sunset, at about six p.m., and it was a good three-hour

151

flight. We were just about to give up hope when Johann came over and gave us the thumbs-up.

We piled the gear into the plane and minutes later we were airborne, flying out across the city and then over an endless canopy of green. Throughout the flight we looked down on forest, broken only by a network of rivers and swamps, and the occasional small logging camp. The sun was low on the horizon when we spied the red patch of bare ground cut into the forest that was Kabo airstrip. Johann was aware he was cutting it fine as far as the light was concerned, especially as he hoped to take off again before dark and fly another 500 kilometres to Franceville, where he would refuel in order to get back to Libreville. I had climbed into the co-pilot's seat for some of the journey and had been amused to see him periodically leaning forward with a big grin and crying out, 'Woo whoa' as we hit another bank of cloud and the plane was buffeted upwards. 'It's just like surfing!' he explained as I raised my eyebrows questioningly.

We came in low for the landing, practically skimming the trees as the light was draining from the sky. It couldn't have been a smoother landing, or a faster turnaround. We grabbed our gear and then waved as the plane roared over our heads and banked steeply, the last rays of the sun glinting on its wings as it turned southwest towards Franceville. A large Renault truck was waiting to take us on to Bomassa, but first we had to clear Customs and Immigration. An Immigration officer and a policeman in immaculate uniforms had appeared from a hut on the edge of the airstrip. Apparently our arrival was quite an event for them and it looked as if they were going to make the most of it. The Immigration officer collected our passports, then disappeared, and the policeman asked us to show him what was in all the cases. First he wanted to investigate a long, suspicious-looking pelican case that belonged to Jake, who opened it to prove that, rather than a rifle, it contained a boom pole for his microphone. Only six years ago in northern Congo there had been a bloody civil war, and the policeman checked the case carefully. Thankfully what he saw inside was sufficiently perplexing to put him off going through the rest, and as soon as we had retrieved our passports we were off.

We bumped down an overgrown logging road with the vegetation pressing in on us and scraping the truck. Sharp-edged vines whipped at the sides, tearing our skin if we didn't duck fast enough. The going was slow, probably no more than about five kilometres an hour, as we rumbled through the night, the headlights creating a pool of light on the muddy track in front of us or sweeping the vegetation as we rounded a bend. Beyond that we could see nothing, except occasional fireflies flickering in the dark forest. We were heading ever deeper into a vast untamed wilderness that explorers once called the Green Hell. We had flown over nearly 1300 kilometres of jungle and it stretched out for hundreds more kilometres in all directions. We were in the middle of nowhere.

Further on the road was blocked by a fallen

tree. The driver hopped out, grabbed a chainsaw from the back of the truck and, by the light of the headlamps, proceeded to cut it up. Having done this many times before, he was proficient and after only twenty minutes we were on our way.

Nearly an hour later Jake said, 'Either there are some humongous fireflies around or we've arrived.' A couple of lights were shining brilliantly through the branches.

I hadn't been at Bomassa for two years but it might as well have been ten minutes because it had changed so little. The research centre is run by the Wildlife Conservation Society (WCS), formerly the New York Zoological Society. Brian Curran and Mark Gately, its directors, were drinking beer in an open-sided hut clad in shorts and T-shirts. They were trying unsuccessfully to discipline a boisterous puppy that had recently adopted them. It was called Mabulu or 'Complete Confusion'. But even having our ankles chewed by pinpoint puppy teeth couldn't detract from the delicious taste of cold beer.

The WCS supports various research projects in northern Congo, most of which are scattered through Nouabale-Ndoki National Park, an area of 4200 square kilometres. Bomassa is a small village just outside the park, on the Sangha river, and this is where the WCS has established its headquarters for supplies and communications. For somewhere so remote it is very up-to-the-minute, with solar panels, a generator, satellite phone and Internet access. Researchers can work there on data and reports. Even more important, after weeks in a basic bush camp they can get a good meal and a warm shower — a cold beer too.

We spent a few days in Bomassa filming around the area and sorting the kit while we waited for James to catch up with us. The small generator that we would be taking with us into the forest clamoured and clattered but refused to produce any charge. Si and Jake tinkered with it — they were in their element: given half a chance they were fixing a bit of equipment or building a rig with some unconventional spare parts. In South America they had once fixed the fuel pump of an old generator with the drip from the first-aid kit. Eventually, however, the obstreperous generator in Bomassa got the better of them and we had to find another.

James arrived a couple of days later. He told us that our first pilot, nice Richard, or his bosses, had invented the problem with the wing flaps: some logging-company bigwigs had been allowed to commandeer the plane. In any contest between them and us, they were bound to win.

'You couldn't help but feel there was some slightly dodgy stuff going on around that place,' James said. When he was due to fly out he'd found his pilot in deep discussion with Richard. The pair were standing in the midday African sun on black sticky tarmac, wearing aviator sun-glasses and talking in Afrikaans. In the background James idly watched a large, squat military transport plane being loaded up with crates and thought, 'Oh God, I'm in a Wilbur Smith novel.'

It was time for us to move on. The area around Bomassa outside the national park is part of a huge logging concession — some 1600 square kilometres. Much of it was felled in 1979 and, although overgrown, it still bears the marks of disturbance so we were keen to get into pristine rainforest. We followed another old logging road for about thirty kilometres as far as Ndoki camp, on the banks of the Ndoki river, which forms the boundary of Nouabale-Ndoki National Park. The camp was empty: it is seldom used and had a sad, abandoned atmosphere — but, then, we too were only passing through. From now on there would be no more roads. The next leg of the journey was by water, which meant transferring all the kit into unstable dugouts.

Luckily we were accompanied by a group of Ba'aka Pygmies, who were skilled at paddling them along the winding waterways, which were no more than a metre or so wide and very shallow. Each canoe had two people paddling: one stood upright at the front, and the other at the back. They constantly had to fend off obstacles in the water or back-paddle to bring the canoe round a bend. We ducked under low, overhanging branches and brushed past ropes of liana that hung trailing into the tea-coloured water. It was wonderfully cool and shady.

Every now and again the canoe rocked as we bumped against a submerged branch or snake-like tree root. As we were burdened with filming equipment, the lip of the canoe was just a couple of centimetres' above the water and a wrong move would tip us all into the river. My camera and computer were wrapped in plastic bags in my ruck-sack, but I was nervous none the less — not so much because I thought we'd capsize but because I'd spotted a small hole spouting a jet of water, which was gradually filling up the bottom of the canoe. I did some bailing with a plastic plate. Mosombo, who was paddling at the front, turned and took in the situation at a glance. He reached out and plucked a thickish stem of grass to plug the hole. Problem solved. The Ba'aka were adept at using the natural materials at hand — as far as they are concerned, they are surrounded by puncture-repair kits, food, tools and medicines, as though the forest were a superstore where everything you could possibly need was readily available.

The Ba'aka possess a unique understanding of the forests of Central Africa and depend on them now as they always have done. No one knows much about their history: few artefacts and traces of ancient peoples survive in the rainforest. What is known is that they have remained separate from other peoples despite extensive migrations throughout the forests of Central Africa. There has been virtually no intermarriage between the Ba'aka and other African peoples because for hundreds, if not thousands, of years the Ba'aka have been regarded as inferior and practically used as slaves. In many places they still are. Governments have done nothing to change this situation, which the Ba'aka meet mostly with resignation.

We joined a wider waterway, the Ndoki river. Flanked by tall trees and lush grass, it looked like a haven for water-birds, but it was utterly quiet and still. Only the steady splash of the paddles going into the water and the gentle bobbing of pale pink waterlilies as our ripples caught them disturbed the calm. Occasionally a dazzling red dragonfly fluttered from its perch on a stem as we went by, to return once we had passed. Everything felt slow and sleepy.

'Do you ever come across elephants here?' I asked Boo.

'Sometimes. They tend to stand around in the middle of the channel, munching, and there's nothing you can do but wait, sometimes for hours.'

As it happened we didn't meet one. I was rather disappointed, but perhaps it was just as well, as we had to reach camp with plenty of time before nightfall if we were going to sort out all the kit. Besides, only about half the stuff had come on the first load and after they dropped us off the canoes would be turning round to go and collect the rest.

We arrived at our destination, Mbeli camp. It is a small research camp, consisting of a couple of wooden huts and some tents, and would be our home for the next couple of weeks. A few research biologists were based there studying forest ecology and gorillas; several Ba'aka trackers were helping them, including Mosombo.

Collectively the Pygmies refer to themselves as Ba'aka or Bayaka, but there are three distinct groups: the Mbuti live in the Ituri forest of the north-eastern Democratic Republic of Congo (DRC); the Twa are scattered throughout the central DRC and in the remaining pockets of forest in Burundi and Rwanda; the BaMbenga inhabit the west of the Congo Basin, where we were, and this group includes several different clans, such as the Babenjele, the Aka, the Babinga and the Ba'ngombe. Both Mosombo and our other helper, Mobaye, were Ba'ngombe. These days, most Ba'aka live in villages, which are rapidly being opened up to the outside world by logging roads, but they return to the forest regularly on hunting and gathering trips, following practices that have been passed down through countless generations. They know the forest like no others.

The forest around Mbeli camp was quite different from that around Bomassa. Enclosed by the trees that loomed over us on all sides, we followed Mosombo in single file. The jungle is intense in every way: you are a stranger stepping into a place of wild things. Overhead, the lattice of thick branches formed a roof blocking out the sun, dark shadows lay between the huge buttress roots, twisted coils of liana hung down in tangles and everywhere the green foliage pressed in. This is one of the least explored places on Earth and it felt like it.

Mosombo remained quiet and moved quickly and freely, weaving through the undergrowth. We had to work hard to keep him in sight — if he got more than a few metres ahead his dull-coloured clothing merged with the vegetation as though he had been swallowed by the forest. No one wants to get lost here and it is easy to do so. A well-known *National Geographic* photographer, and old friend of mine, Nick Nichols, got lost and the story is retold regularly around Mbeli. Nick has spent a lot of time in forests and is pretty bushwise, but after he told his Pygmy tracker that he and his son could find their own way to '12k' camp in the Gualogo, a region to the east of Mbeli, they were lost before they had gone 300 metres. In rainforest your sense of direction deserts you in minutes: every tree starts to look the same, in every direction a tangle of green presents itself, and often you cannot even see the sun to orientate yourself. At sunset they had to face the prospect of sleeping out in the forest, burning a novel to keep animals away. Thankfully they were tracked down the following day: Nick was able to call Bomassa on his satellite phone, although he couldn't tell anyone where they were.

At times as we walked through the forest I found myself behind Mosombo: as he wove through the vegetation he snapped back the tips of small branches at waist-to-eye height every few metres. I don't think he thought about it — it was second nature to him to mark his path through the forest so that he could find his way back. When I glanced back, the trail of broken stems was far from conspicuous, but for Mosombo it was probably as obvious as a large arrow on a road.

We had been walking for several hours and had seen nothing. We could have been forgiven for thinking that the place was empty of animals, but we knew that was not the case. There *were* animals and, no doubt, they were watching us, interlopers passing through their domain.

The animals of this underworld are adapted for life in the half-light. Thousands of species camouflage themselves or have physiques that echo the surrounding foliage. In the underworld, you can never be certain that a leaf or a twig is just that: if you watch patiently, in time much of the vegetation comes to life. A line of leaves might be a collection of leaf bugs, a twig could be a stick insect, and that pile of dead leaves on the forest floor, a cricket.

Or course, camouflage is as effective at hiding predators as it is at hiding prey. In the Congo, many predators use ambush rather than pursuit to catch their dinner because, in dense vegetation, pursuit is dangerous and difficult. The Congo's top predator, the leopard, has a special 'forest edition' coat, much darker than that of its relatives on the open plains. The rainforest is the only location in which the leopard's black coloration is common — there, being part of the shadows has its advantages.

Snakes are especially well camouflaged: the gaboon viper moves through the leaf litter under a patterned cloak of brown; the black coils of a spitting cobra blend with the shadows among the roots of giant trees; and even the thick body of a puff adder lies perfectly concealed among dead leaves. You rarely see snakes when walking through the forest and, if you do, you realise how easy it would be to brush past them unawares. I have had many close encounters with snakes in forests, but I know that the ones I've seen are just a fraction of those that have seen me.

It is so hard to see anything in the forest that hearing is the predominant sense in many animals: when walking through the forest you can easily slip into a trance listening to its many voices. Louis Sarno is an American anthropologist who has spent seventeen years living in the area with the Ba'aka and has grown to know the forest almost as well as they do. In *Bayaka: The Extraordinary Music of the Babenzélé Pygmies*, he writes, 'Above all it's the sounds of the forest that I tune, not merely to my ears, but to my entire being . . . The most basic electronic pulse which never ceases is composed of legions of tireless insects.' Cicadas are the most evident, producing high-pitched blasts of white noise that can drive you to distraction. But, as Sarno points out,

No sound is more evocative of the forest, and when the Bayaka hear the voice of the *elele* [cicadas] they say it makes their heart glad.

To the rasps, chirps, whirs and clicks of the Orthoptera [grasshoppers, crickets, katydids] and Homoptera [cicadas, aphids, etc.] must be added the steady hum of the Diptera, Hymenoptera and Coleoptera — the fly, bee and beetle kingdoms. They buzz in the air absolutely everywhere. On the next level are the twitters, peeps, warbles, coos and chirrups of the little birds — the bulbuls, shrikes, trogons, cuckoos, orioles and many others. These are sounds that come and go but are seldom completely absent . . . Then there are the larger birds and many of the mammals. Their voices are so distinctive that close up they always strongly mark the moment of their occurrence, distinguishing it from the moments before and after.

Given the orchestra of forest sounds it is not surprising that the Ba'aka are primarily aural rather than visual people. They are acutely aware of noises and use subtle sound-maps, created by the murmuring of streams and the calls of territorial birds and mammals, to locate themselves. They play with sound too, whistling, calling and singing to keep in touch, and make musical instruments from anything to hand — water, a tree root or a hollow stem.

Mobaye showed us how to make a *geedal* or bow harp. Using a machete, he cut a straight stem of wood nearly a metre long, then pulled down several metres of liana, which he coiled over his shoulder like a rope. He stripped away the outer layer of the liana, leaving just a long strip of the inner pith, about five millimetres in diameter. This would form the harp strings, and he cut it into three precise lengths. He sliced a notch half-way along the wooden stem, into which he fitted a small piece of wood to act as a bridge with three more notches in it to hold the three strings, then stretched the strings across the bridge and bound them to either end of the wooden stem, to make a wide, triangular harp.

Later that evening we sat around the fire with the Ba'aka and listened to songs about the forest. Mobaye had dried out his harp by the fire and it was now resting on his knee as he plucked the strings with both hands. Mosombo, in charge of the tempo, tapped a bottle with a spoon while we clapped in rhythm. They sang about a hunter who turned himself into a mouse so that he could sneak up on an elephant. When he got close he turned back into a man and shot it.

The relationship between Ba'aka and forest is complex. Traditionally they regard the forest as their parent, for it is their provider. On the other hand they fear the powerful and sometimes malevolent forest spirits, who remind people of their debt to the forest as their source of life. After witnessing an elephant hunt Kevin Duffy, an anthropologist who lived with and filmed the Mbuti of the Ituri forest, wrote that 'after killing the animal they pray over its body and pray for themselves because they believe what they did is wrong'.

Ba'aka society is egalitarian: men and women are equal and there are no chiefs or shamans. The supreme god is Kumba, the creator of all things; some say he has taken powers from animals and given them to people. Unlike most other belief systems, Kumba is not actively worshipped and is rather removed from day-to-day life. Much more direct influence is exerted by the powerful and sometimes malevolent forest spirits. Spirits, such as the *bobe*, are never far away, reminding people of their presence with screams and cries at dawn or passing through camp in the dead of night. 'Sometimes the lively chatter in camp in late afternoon will momentarily fall silent at the sharp report of a popping leaf from the surrounding forest, a sure indication of Bobe's presence,' Louis Sarno writes. They are invoked with drumming and singing in a ceremony called *boyobi* when the Ba'aka make their hunting camps in the forest. In the villages *boyobi* is also performed as a much larger ceremony at which whole neighbourhoods come together. 'During these ceremonies the magic is evident. [The village] seems to be floating in its own private dimension; usually a mist isolates it from the rest of the world. The music itself is vast and wild and sometimes stunningly complex.'

The song Mosombo and the others sang next was about Ejengi, the most powerful of all the forest spirits. When a number of boys are regarded as ready for initiation into manhood, Ejengi manifests himself at night as a giant covered in leaves and grasses, dancing through a village in a ceremony that can go for months. On some days there will be a lull in the music; on others almost continuous drumming and song. Mobaye explained that Ejengi was very dangerous: he steals people and takes them into the forest to kill them. Yet he also nurtures and protects. The forest is the provider, but it is also a source of fear.

If you take a few paces from the fire and step into the forest at night, you feel disoriented almost immediately: the trees and branches form strange shadows, vines and roots are twisted and

165

coiled like snakes, and behind them there is nothing but gaping darkness. If you turn off your torch it is utterly black. No moonlight penetrates the canopy: this is one of the darkest places on earth. You pick up the scent of damp leaves or flowers, and hear the constant sighing and rustling of branches and falling leaves. Every now and then a twig snaps or an animal cries. The tree hyrax, a small animal about the size of a rabbit whose closest relative is, curiously, the elephant, shrieks like a banshee, producing an unearthly sound. They are almost impossible to detect in the branches and it is easy to see how their disembodied calls would fuel stories of spirits.

During the day you experience the sensation that you are being watched, and at night it is markedly heightened. The forest seems to be more than the sum of its parts — it has a presence that goes beyond the trees and animals, which may explain why the notion of forest spirits runs through so many diverse cultures. But there may be something more deep-rooted too: while the jungle is an alien place, it is likely that it was where humans first evolved and developed our most basic, instinctive fears. The sense of clandestine creatures and hidden forces at work may even have produced the first whisperings of human spiritual beliefs.

As we continued to explore the forest around camp, we were struck by how varied the forest can be. Sometimes we entered vegetation so dense we could barely swing a machete. I tried my hand at cutting through the tangle of vines and undergrowth, swinging the heavy blade back and forth, aiming low and trying to find a steady rhythm, but progress was much faster when I handed the machete back to Mosombo. From an early age the Ba'aka handle knives with extraordinary skill — which is not surprising when you see the casual way in which tiny toddlers play with them. I once saw a little boy of about four hacking at a piece of firewood with a machete; there were no adults nearby, just a few dogs lazing in the shade. On another occasion James took a photograph of three little girls sitting in a row, each with a *Crocodile Dundee*-sized knife resting in her lap.

As we trudged along, we would point out a flash of colour or some bizarre foamy white fungus, a spotted mushroom or a bright yellow one trumpeted like a chanterelle, but mostly we were hypnotised by the tracery of the vines and branches overhead. Contrary to what you might expect, the deeper into pristine forest you go, the more open the understorey becomes. When you look up, the canopy forms a closed green ceiling above you, blocking out the sun. Barely 2 per cent of the light energy hitting the roof of the forest penetrates to its floor, which means that, on average, this underworld is illuminated by the equivalent of a 10- or 20-watt bulb. Yet in this dim world hundreds of plant species find enough light energy to grow.

Plants employ every possible trick to catch the available sunlight, and while it seemed that we were surrounded by a chaotic tangle of vegetation, it was nothing of the sort. The plants arrange their leaves with great care, sometimes in rows, sometimes in rosettes, but always so that no leaf overlaps another. The leaves are flat and large, like solar panels, laid out horizontally to maximise their ability to trap light. Some go a step further and grow leaves with cells that act as prisms, directing the light towards the chief photosynthesising cells.

Even with these adaptations, though, life below the canopy is unprofitable. Plants in the shade do not have the energy of the canopy trees. There are only the tiniest margins between the amount of light energy captured by the plant and the amount of energy needed to survive, and growth is slow: a seedling a mere 10 centimetres tall may be as much as thirty years old.

But these saplings are adapted to life in the gloomy underworld. In their early years they are capable of germinating only in the shade. They spend their infancy under the canopy in a semi-dormant form, sometimes for decades, growing very slowly or not at all. During this time they invest in the quality of their wood, laying down dense, reinforced tissues, an essential foundation for trees that may eventually weigh over 100 tonnes. Unfortunately their quality is highly prized by the outside world. Built to last, these hardwoods are the perfect materials for superior furniture. It is ironic that these plants, the most sought-after by the timber companies, should also be the ones that are most vulnerable to the long-term effects of logging: they fail to generate in clear-felled, sun-baked land, and are also the slowest-growing of the rainforest's trees.

Nature can't do much about timber companies, but most of the trees can at least protect themselves against being eaten. The Barteria tree grows to 5–10 metres, with thin branches and huge leaves. I snipped off the end of a branch with secateurs. Less than a second later, a stream of ants poured out of the hollow stem; within minutes the whole tree was swarming with angry insects. These are Tetrapoenera and their vicious bite injects poison. From personal experience I know that it is very painful. In Gabon the barteria is called the adulteress tree: apparently, women who have been unfaithful to their husbands are tied to it as punishment.

Other plants defend themselves with spines or sharp hairs. The manniophyton looks innocent but it is like glass sandpaper and will strip off your skin if you brush past it. Others contain chemicals such as tannins and lignins, which make the leaves unpalatable or indigestible. A few contain poisons, alkaloids that can kill — Strychnos, for instance, contains strychnine, as its name suggests. The toxins evolved to prevent animals eating the leaves, but they are also potent medicines for those who know how to use them.

One day, singing, laughing and calling to each other, the Ba'aka women went into the forest at our request to gather medicinal plants. They bundled together armfuls of different species, but when I asked them — through Fafa, our camp cook — what they were for they laughed and said they weren't for anything but they might look good on television! It turned out, however, that they had gathered practically an entire pharmacy. They had plants for common ailments, such as stomach upsets, headaches, fever and rashes, one that helped breast-feeding mothers produce milk, another that was good for heart disease and even some bark from the yohimbe tree, which, they explained, would give a man an erection for a week.

A quarter of all medicines available in the world today owe their existence to plants. More than two thousand varieties of tropical plant are thought to contain chemicals that will combat cancer; others attack viruses, including HIV, asthma, rheumatoid arthritis, rheumatic fever, heart disease, malaria, tetanus or glaucoma, or act as sedatives, stimulants, tranquillisers and anti-depressants. Two alkaloids from the leaves of the rosy periwinkle from Madagascar are used to treat childhood leukaemia with a 99 per cent chance that the disease will go into remission. Before rosy periwinkle was used as a treatment for Hodgkin's disease there was virtually no hope for patients: now there is a 90 per cent chance of survival. The list goes on and on, yet so far only 1 per cent of rainforest plants have been properly examined for their medical potential. Let's hope we don't destroy this living medicine chest before we know its true value.

It is not just the Ba'aka but also the animals in the forest who are aware of these plants' medicinal properties — red colobus monkeys use cyanide from Prunus trees to get rid of gut parasites, while bonobos, eastern lowland gorilla and chimpanzees have been observed using other plants medicinally. Chimps may use as many as sixteen different medicinal plants, one of which is a herbaceous plant called *Vernonia amygdalina*. This is taken more during the wet season when parasite infections are at their highest. Field researchers such as Mike Huffman of Kyoto University in Japan observed ill chimpanzees chewing the bitter pith of *Vernonia amygdalina*. When they looked at the chimpanzees' dung afterwards they found that the infection of parasites such as nematodes, trematodes and protozoae had dropped noticeably. Chemical analyses revealed that these plants contain steroids and other chemicals with antiparasitic activity. How chimpanzees first learned that a plant with virtually no nutritional benefit could be of service in other ways is a mystery but once a chimpanzee has learned to distinguish between harmful plants and those that have beneficial properties, this behaviour is passed on to others allowing the whole group to benefit from the experience of an individual. Interestingly the WaTongwe people from Tanzania also use the same plant as a treatment for stomach aches and parasite infections.

Another type of medicinal plant use in chimps involves swallowing leaves whole. I've watched them roll a leaf up with their tongues and swallow it in one with determined expressions. Mike Huffman found that when swallowing leaves whole, chimpanzees are not benefiting from any chemicals within the leaves, rather the leaves are acting mechanically to purge the chimps of parasites. The leaves have a rough surface covered with short hairs which trap parasites as they pass through the gut. A new form of medication that has never been documented among humans.

The eldest and most playful of the Ba'aka women was called Apumu. She and I had a conversation in mime: I pointed to a plant and Apumu would pat her stomach vigorously, or stage a shivering fever and convulsions, or double over in a coughing fit. Nigel persuaded Fafa to ask the women to prepare a medicine that I could try for the film. 'Maybe something for a stomach upset,' he said.

I didn't feel any need for treatment in that department, but was prepared to try anything. Apumu picked up her machete and started chopping some leaves into a bowl of water, then pounded and stirred the mixture. I pointed to my stomach and looked at her questioningly. She shook her head, then embraced herself and put her arm up making a strongman fist. 'She says it is not for stomachache, it just makes you feel good,' Fafa translated.

'Great,' I said. 'That's exactly what I need.'

When the water was dark green, Apumu scooped up a cupful and drank it, then scooped up another and handed it to me. It tasted fine, if a little bitter.

Boo looked closely at the leaves. 'I wouldn't drink too much, Charlotte,' she said. 'I don't know exactly what it is, but it belongs to the *Apocynaceae*, a family of plants that contain

172

cyanide and alkaloids and might be pretty potent.'

I had about half a cupful and about twenty minutes later felt quite lively and awake, although it was the end of a long day. I noticed that my heart-rate had increased a little, but there were no other apparent physical or mental effects. It was, as Nigel gleefully noted, the perfect 'Pygmy up'.

8

When Giants Die

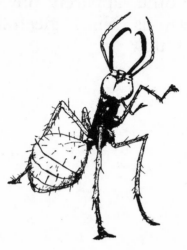

As the days went by at Mbeli it got progressively hotter and more humid until we could barely think or move. Tasks that should have taken five minutes lasted hours. We were plagued by millions of tiny black sweat bees: they are stingless, but still capable of driving you mad. They come in droves to drink your sweat, getting under your shirt and tickling your skin, crawling all over your arms and neck until you are furry with them. They hover millimetres from your face, climb up your nose and into your eyes. 'I hate the way they get into my ears,' Si said, 'and I can feel their little feet marching about in there.'

Black clouds of them hovered over the equipment and millions more crawled over the handles, which were moist with sweat. Salts are rare in the forest, and a hot, sweaty film crew was a rich discovery.

When we weren't filming, I would find a tree trunk to lean against and catch up with notes for the book.

'Are we going to be in it?' Si asked.

'Have I saved the day yet?' Jake asked, peering over my shoulder. 'Perhaps you could put in, 'Luckily there's Jake — he'll rescue me . . . ''

'Have *I* saved the day?' James enquired.

I shook my head. 'No, you've all been hopeless, I'm afraid.'

But I sometimes found that mysterious hands had been at work when I left my notebook unattended on the ground. There were little additions, slipped surreptitiously between the lines which read, 'and then Jake saved the day!'

One evening I was sitting outside my tent at my computer, trying to get my brain in gear to write up my notes and desperately trying to figure out how to work Jake in as a hero, but it was too hot to concentrate. A platoon of tiny ants filed over the ground towards me. I watched them absent-mindedly and then abruptly sprang to my feet slapping my leg in response to a stingingly painful bite. Hot and hounded by ants, I gave up and wandered over to a nearby log where I settled down and opened *Travels in West Africa* by Mary Kingsley. This is the extraordinary story of an eccentric Englishwoman's journeys alone through the Congo at the end of the nineteenth century. Apparently when she told an acquaintance who had been to the region that she intended on going alone to West Africa he had said

'When you have made up your mind to go to West Africa the very best thing you can do is get it unmade again and go to Scotland instead; but if your intelligence is not strong enough to do so, abstain from exposing yourself to the direct rays of the sun, take 4 grains of quinine every day for a fortnight before you reach the Rivers and get some introductions to the Wesleyans; they are the only people on the Coast who have got a hearse with feathers.'

Undeterred she went, armed with collecting jars and bags as she was in her own words 'a beetle and fetish hunter'. In her introduction to the book Elspeth Huxley writes

'These journeys were remarkable not for any geographical discoveries . . . Rather they were remarkable because the traveller, a sheltered middle-class Victorian spinster lady of no unusual appearance, without protection, without knowledge of African languages, who had probably never even slept in a tent on the lawn, went entirely alone into regions . . . where a solitary unprotected female without possessions, travelling on foot was an open invitation to be . . . eaten like any stray wild beast.'

I wiped the beads of sweat from my forehead. How she had coped with traipsing through the forest in full length skirt and starched blouse I couldn't imagine but reading her account it is obvious that what kept her going was not only an indomitable spirit but also a great sense of humour.

'There are an abominable lot of bees around; they do not give one a moment's peace, getting beneath waterproof sheets over the bed, and pretending they can't get out and forthwith losing their tempers, which is imbecile, because the whole four sides of the affair are broad open ... I confess I don't feel up to much hunting after yesterdays work, but deem it advisable to rest. My face and lips are a misery to me, having been blistered all over by yesterday's sun, and last night I whipped the skin all off one cheek with the blanket, and it keeps on bleeding, and horror of horrors, there is no tea until that water comes.'

She was rapidly becoming a hero of mine. Elsewhere she writes

'To my taste there is nothing so fascinating as spending a night out in an African forest, or plantation; but I beg you to note I do not advise anyone to follow the practice. Nor indeed do I recommend African forest life to anyone. Unless you are interested in it and fall under its charm it is the most awful life in death imaginable. It is like being shut up in a library whose books you cannot read all the while tormented [and] terrified . . . And if you do fall under its spell it takes the colour out of other kinds of living. Still, it is good for a man to have experience of it, whether he likes it or not, for it teaches you how very independent you have been, during your previous life, on the familiarity of those conditions you have been brought up among, and on your fellow citizens; moreover it takes the conceit out of you pretty thoroughly during the days you spend stupidly stumbling about among your new surroundings.'

I heard an explosive 'piaou' followed by movement in the trees and I got up to watch a group of white-nosed monkeys feeding in the branches overhead their tails dangling down like streamers. In the distance there was the occasional rumble of thunder and I silently pleaded with the gods just to get on with it and let it rip. Sometimes you hear thunder and then the storm passes you by, but this time the humidity had reached fever pitch and there simply had to be a break in the weather.

Finally after dusk the wind was rustling the leaves in the treetops and I heard the splash of fat raindrops on the leaves around me. I gathered up my papers and computer, then dived into the tent. Within minutes it had become a downpour. I stripped off and charged outside to dance in it. It was one of the most refreshing showers ever:

the temperature had dropped a staggering 7° from 32° to 25° Celsius in about ten minutes. I love the energy of tropical storms. Moments later there was an ear-splitting boom, as though heavy artillery had just been fired. The sound echoed again and again through the forest and I felt the ground vibrate. A giant tree had crashed down.

Not long ago a visitor to Mbeli had a close shave when a branch came down on her tent and crushed it — fortunately she wasn't inside it at the time. Every day in the rainforest several large branches come down, and frequently whole trees. They are often battered by raging storms and even on sunny days constant winds buffet the canopy 30 metres above. Although you might expect that the titanic trees of tropical rainforests have long life-spans, compared to temperate trees they don't: this is a much more dynamic environment in which trees, the architecture of the forest, are replaced every 80–135 years.

Nevertheless, the death of a tree is a big event. When a 100-tonne tree comes down, it flattens everything in its path. It also punctures a massive hole in the canopy — a 'light gap'. As the sunlight floods to the forest floor it brings about startling changes. In an area the size of a tennis court as many as 60,000 seeds may be waiting for this moment and there is an explosion of growth. Plants race for the light and hardwood seedlings that have been semi-dormant for decades are awakened. This isn't just a chaotic proliferation of plants, it is a highly organised reaction, and ecologists are just beginning to understand the patterns of change that a tree's

179

plunge sets in motion.

Different-sized light gaps nurture different kinds of plants. A big tree falling will create a large gap, because it is usually lashed to its neighbours by lianas and will take others down with it; when a whole stand of trees comes down — perhaps due to a landslide or fire — the gaps can be huge, but this is rare so the seeds that must take advantage of a sudden burst of light have to be ready. Most plants that invade these areas produce large quantities of fruit packed with tiny seeds, which are dispersed by birds and bats in a scattergun approach; this increases the probability of a seed being in the right place when a gap in the canopy appears. Whether in South East Asia, the Amazon or Africa, I discovered pioneer trees are of a strikingly similar design. To be successful they must be able to withstand strong sun and heavy rain: they have large leaves, they grow fast, die young (at about eighty years) and are often structurally 'cheap' — for example, they may have hollow stems.

The smallest light gaps occur when a single limb or a small tree comes down. As this happens frequently, the species that can take advantage of it produce fewer, large seeds that are dispersed less widely. Larger seeds enable root systems to develop rapidly; they also store carbohydrate reserves that nourish the seedlings as they wait for a gap to appear. Then they race up to fill the space. Ecologists used to think of rainforests as stable, but in fact the relentless tree-falls produce a dynamic ecosystem, an ever-changing mosaic of variously filled light gaps. In turn these create an endless variety of different habitats for animals. When a tree falls it brings with it to the forest floor living leaves, fruit and seeds that are a bonanza to animals such as pigs and deer. But even after these delicacies have been finished the explosion of plant growth continues to provide flowers, fruit and seeds.

The morning after the storm when everything had calmed down, we walked into a clearing where two trees lay. As we emerged from the gloomy forest into the blazing sun, we immediately attracted the dreaded sweat bees. I did my best to ignore them and sat down on one of the fallen trees to look around. These trees had come down during a previous storm, producing a medium-sized light gap. Around my feet there was already a thick carpet of fresh green seedlings, a mixture of pioneers and canopy trees. In a hundred years' time some would form the great pillars of the forest. They had light, they had water; now all they needed was nutrients from the soil. When you look at the profusion of vegetation in every direction it seems clear that the soil in the rainforest is every gardener and farmer's dream — rich, thick and fertile — but if you scrape away the dead leaves, you will find just a few millimetres of earth. Below that there is a sandy desert. Although the fallen giant I was sitting on must once have stood about seventy metres high, its roots were only about fifty centimetres long — nothing compared to the vast root systems of temperate

181

trees. This is typical of rainforest trees: there is simply not enough soil to put down extensive root systems. It is one of the reasons why they come down in storms and perhaps why they produce large buttresses at the base of their trunks to stabilise them.

That the richest ecosystem on Earth is founded on a bed of shallow soil is one of the greatest surprises about rainforests. But why should this be so, and how can soil like this support so much plant life?

In this case, the answer to life is death. Nothing in the rainforest goes to waste, and everything is recycled with unimaginable efficiency. Without this the forest ecosystem would quickly collapse. As soon as a tree comes down, vast armies of recyclers get to work, taking nutrients into the underworld, the forest's secret power plant. It's a place that, for sheer variety, puts the Serengeti to shame: a handful of soil contains up to 50 billion creatures belonging to more than a million different species.

In this miniature universe there are animals and plants, vegetarians and carnivores, predators and prey just as there are in the large-scale version. The microflora consist of some 35,000 species of fungi and a host of bacteria, possibly 20–40,000 species in every gram of soil. They are crucial in fixing elements such as nitrogen, sulphur and iron into a form that other organisms can handle. They are also demolition experts. Wood contains lignin and cellulose, both of which are hard to break down. Lignin, in particular, is so tough that only fungi and bacteria equipped with special enzymes can digest it. We are familiar with the fruiting bodies of fungi when they sprout as mushrooms and toadstools, but the main part of a fungus lies below ground, a vast intricate web of micro-scopic hair-like *hyphae*, stretching out under the forest floor. This fungal network is what starts to break down the wood.

The animal life in this Lilliputian kingdom comprises about 40,000 different species of protozoa and more than 100,000 different nematodes, which graze on the fungi and bacteria, making carbon and nitrogen available to larger organisms. Higher up the food chain are more nematodes, mites and ants that prey on other soil animals and parasites, and at the very top are terrifying predators such as centipedes.

Of all the soil animals, termites are probably the most important to the process of recycling. As the tree starts to rot, the lignin is broken down by the bacteria and fungi, then wood-eating termites move in, attacking the cellulose. And it's not just trees that need to be recycled: in the rainforest there is a steady drip, drip, drip of nutrients falling to the floor — a leaf drops every 15–20 seconds. Termites alone are responsible for breaking up 30 per cent of all of this waste matter and you can often hear them at work under the leaf litter, a steady rasping sound coming in waves. While for a tree the process of demolition and recycling can take 15–20 years, the leaf litter will have decomposed within just six weeks.

Then other types of termite get going,

subterranean creatures that condition the soil by making holes through which gases and water can pass, and by releasing carbon and sticky compounds that help to bind the soil together. Now it is ready for new plants.

But giant trees need extra help and they get it from a surprising quarter: a group of fungi called Mycorrhizae. If you turn over a rotting leaf in the forest carefully you may find fine white threads travelling from it into the ground. Although we can barely see them, they form part of an extensive filigree of gossamer-thin threads that interlock with the roots of trees and deliver nutrients from dead matter directly into the roots. In return they receive a tiny amount of sunshine in a supply of sugars from the tree.

The very idea that these giant trees rely on such a delicate network of underground threads is astonishing, but it is the efficiency with which the relationship allows trees to take up nutrients that makes the soil of the rainforest so poor. There is absolutely no slack in the system: as soon as a twig, leaf, flower, branch or even dead animal falls to the ground it is immediately taken back into the living forest in a never-ending cycle of death, decay and regeneration. And, ultimately, this is what makes the rainforests so rich: at any given moment, almost all of the available energy is bound up in the living system, and particularly in the trees. This makes rainforests fragile: remove trees, and soon there is nothing to put back in to allow the forest to regenerate. In many parts of the world where forest has been cleared for agriculture it is difficult to scratch a meagre crop from land where once a lush forest grew.

Most ancient 'jungle' civilisations adopted slash-and-burn agriculture, in which small plots of forest were cut down and burned. The clearings were used for a couple of years, then left fallow for about twenty to recover before they were used again. At low population levels — of about fifty people per square kilometre — this is sustainable, but as populations increased more and more forest was cleared and fallow time reduced to squeeze more harvests from the land. This quickly became unsustainable, and was probably the reason for the dramatic collapse of the Mayan civilisation in Central America and contributed to the fall of the Khmer Empire in Cambodia. Now only overgrown jungle temples remain as a reminder of former greatness. It should be a sobering lesson for us today.

You don't have to spend long in the forest to realise that the smallest creatures play an essential role in maintaining it. The floor is populated by an extraordinary array of them, especially insects. Nigel found a bizarre creature, half the size of my little fingernail, crawling over his shoe: it had a triangular black body, six legs sporting flaps like baggy trousers, and white-striped antennae. On another occasion a tiny, bright scarlet spider with jet-black legs abseiled to the ground next to us.

Most insects are small and inconspicuous, but some are impossible to miss. The Goliath beetle is a massive 12 centimetres long and makes a loud humming in flight. As Cuthbert Christy wrote in his 1952 book, *La Grande Chasse au pays des Pygmées*, 'The illusion is not lessened when he descends in wide circles to land . . . the sound of humming diminishes and the speed reduces. Then, the large claws with their formidable hooks for anchoring take hold . . . and the wings are brought together their hinged sails folded orderly from below . . . One would almost expect to see a passenger get out.'

The insects that you notice most, however, are those that bite. It was for good reason that early explorers referred to these forests as the Green Hell. In addition to the oppressive heat and humidity, you are constantly attacked by mosquitoes, tsetse flies, filaria flies — all of which leave you with itchy or painful bites, sometimes infections and occasionally a parting gift of parasites. Mosquitoes carry malaria, tsetse flies carry sleeping sickness and filaria flies carry filariasis, a parasite that passes across your eyeball during its lifecycle. This, locals say, is the moment to grab it and get rid of it.

We tend to think of wildlife in terms of obvious animals, but the majority of living creatures on our planet are insects, maybe some 10 million different species. In the rainforest they fill every possible niche. Around the world, the rainforests' greatest predators are not leopards or tigers but ants, and in Africa the most awe-inspiring are the driver or siafu ants.

Driver ants form colonies 22 million strong and head off from a central bivouac to carry out devastating raids on the forest around them. If ever there was a spectacle in nature that seemed to be drawn straight from the realms of science fiction, this is it. Column after column of worker ants surge through the leaf litter, impelled by potent pheromones, rushing over the top of each other in their frenzy to reach the front — a relentless living river moving as a single giant organism. Flanking the main column fiendish-looking soldier ants stand poised, their mandibles open and ready to attack anything that comes to disturb the marching line. If you are unlucky enough to walk into a column they break ranks and swarm. Within seconds they are crawling all over you, delivering savage bites to your legs, arms, torso and head. They even crawl into your hair and bite. Often you have no choice but to run into the forest, strip and shake them out. Even the little ones give a painful nip, but the soldiers can draw blood and in their millions they can kill you. There are awful stories of people falling down drunk in the forest and being eaten alive, and even of the ants being used as a horrendous form of execution by colonialists in the former Belgian Congo.

Getting close enough to film them wasn't easy. The army is sensitive to movement and vibration. so we crept up on them through the undergrowth as though we were playing Grandmother's Footsteps. It was no good: every time we got close some ants would leave the column to swarm around us, and by the time we'd leapt about in an effort to get them out of our clothes the whole column was seething across the ground. We had no choice but to beat a speedy retreat. In the end we put on our wellies and wrapped yards of gaffer-tape, sticky side out, round the tops of our boots with an extra ring round the ankle for good measure. This proved to be a virtually foolproof way of getting into the fray without being savaged.

We followed the army back to their bivouac, an area of about four square metres distinguished by the fresh red earth that lay over it. Dotted across its surface but concentrated at the main entrance holes were more soldiers. A disturbing smell of rotting flesh emanated from it: the carnage from previous assaults on the area. Beneath us was a closely guarded underground bunker where soldiers link their bodies together to form a living barricade. At the heart of the subterranean city is the inner sanctum where the queen resides. She is the largest ant on earth, a living egg-machine producing 100,000 a day. Up to 2.5 million ant eggs and larvae are nurtured in the bivouac at one time, but this is not only a massive nursery: it is also the base of operations and the launch station for the vast campaigns that provide vital supplies for the colony.

Not long afterwards we had first-hand experience of one of these forays: the ants paid us a visit in camp. James woke to the sound of scratching and opened his eyes to find that the inside wall of the flysheet was one dark, seething mass of ants. Time to make a sharp exit. The ants had spread out from their orderly columns and swarmed through camp, forming a moving carpet. We grabbed our boots and ran for it, then watched awestruck from a safe distance as the tents were subsumed and the hut was taken over. All around us, the ground came alive with spiders, grasshoppers, cicadas, lizards and butterflies fleeing from the ants; moths and cockroaches rained down from the roof of the hut in a desperate bid to escape the marching millions that climbed the walls. Nothing was safe unless it had wings and used them fast. Some say even elephants will run when driver ants are on the move.

The majority of the animals didn't make it. As soon as a few ants got hold of an unfortunate creature, its struggles brought in more until all that was visible was a mound of writhing ants. The drivers are the cleaners of the forest: every bit of debris and every animal they find is dragged back to the bivouac. To us it looked like an invasion of aliens in a horror film.

On one of our last nights in Mbeli we were having supper in the communal hut, beads of sweat glistening on our brows and upper lips. It was stiflingly hot and humid again and it didn't let up even at night. The subject of food often cropped up around the table. The nearest shop was nearly two days travel (much later we discovered that it was actually a small stall selling a limited but eclectic selection of merchandise — soap, cigarettes, sugar, batteries and ginger), and with no electricity or fridge, fresh food lasted no time at all. Dinner was usually sardines and rice and, when things got bad, it was some rancid-smelling dried fish that was re-hydrated into an unappetising sludge, and fou-fou, a glutinous dough-like stuff made out of manioc (cassava).

Unsurprisingly, Mary Kingsley had had something to say on the subject of fou-fou as well and she hadn't been crazy about it either.

'This manioc meal is the staple food, the bread equivalent, all along the coast. As you pass along you are perpetually meeting with a new named food, fou-fou on the Leeward, kank on the Windward, m'vada in Corisco, agooma in the Ogowe; but acquaintance with it demonstrates that it is all the same — manioc. If I ever meet a tribe that refers to buttered muffins I shall know what to expect and so not get excited.'

Angela, one of the researchers at Mbeli, had been there for three and a half years studying western lowland gorillas, and told us a story about the special treat she and her colleagues had awarded themselves one Christmas. They had bought a duck, which waddled around the camp waiting for the fateful day. Suddenly it disappeared. It might have been taken by a civet, or got lost in the forest, but the researchers' suspicions were aroused a few days later when someone from the nearby village appeared with a duck that looked remarkably similar to the first. As they had no way of proving that it was indeed their duck they had no choice but to buy it again.

This evening the food was exceptionally good:

rice, plantain bananas and a sauce of tinned sardines and tinned peas. The rice sat on the table in a large white enamelled pot with a picture on it of some proud leader in military attire, flanked on one side by a city of skyscrapers and on the other a crest.

'Who is this on the pot, Boo?' Nigel asked. 'Is it Sassou-Ngessou, [the President of western Congo]?'

Boo peered at it, then asked someone to pass her a torch. 'No,' she said. 'It's not Sassou-Ngessou, or Biya [the President of Cameroon], or even Bozize [of the Central African Republic]. It's generic dictatorware!'

In a part of the world where leaders change with more regularity than David Beckham's hairstyles it makes eminently good sense to produce memorabilia to suit all situations.

The conversation moved on to gorillas and then to elephants, both of which live in the forest and which we were hoping to film at our next destination. Thomas, a German who had arrived about six months ago to take over as research co-ordinator, told us of their trials with a rogue elephant who occasionally caused havoc. His name was Andy, or Le Bandit. Once, they had left the camp over Christmas and he had trashed the place: they came back to a half-collapsed kitchen, hut doors hanging off their hinges, clothes strewn everywhere. He had even eaten their precious collection of magazines and books, leaving just a few torn pages.

'I couldn't sleep for the first few nights I was here — I couldn't even pluck up the courage to go out to the loo in the night. It was awful,' said Lyndsay, who had arrived a couple of months previously.

'Still, we shouldn't complain,' Angela said. 'It's nothing compared to what it's like at Dzanga and Bai Hoku, where the researchers have it really bad — their camps are always being invaded by bad-tempered elephants.'

That was where we were going next.

⋆ ⋆ ⋆

Dzanga and Bai Hoku are situated in the south-western tip of the Central African Republic (CAR), a thin triangle jutting out between Congo and Cameroon. To get there we had to go up the Sangha river, which forms the boundary between CAR, Congo and Cameroon. We set off in canoes with small outboard motors. On the Cameroon side a fisherman stood in his boat casting his net. As he threw it upwards into the air it fanned out like a shimmering web, the trees of the bank visible for a moment through the translucent mesh, before it hit the water in a wide arc. At times progress was slow as our boatmen had to go carefully for fear that the engine propeller might run aground. It was the beginning of the wet season, so the river was low, only about a metre deep. Often we stayed close to one side or the other where the channels seemed deeper and passed floating islands of deep green water plants with spikes of lilac-coloured flowers — water hyacinth. It is pretty, but a terrible invader, from South

America, that is working its way round the world, taking over and choking rivers.

Occasionally there was a little clearing on the bank, a small homestead with dogs, chickens and wooden houses on stilts, the universal design used to cope with flooding, whether it be in South East Asia, Amazonia or central Africa. As we passed, small gangs of children burst out on to the riverbank screaming and waving at us in frantic excitement, and once an old man hurried over, raising his arm in greeting and grinning from ear to ear.

Even steering close to the edge we went aground every now and then, the jolt rocking the canoe so violently that we almost fell out. Eventually we arrived at a small village called Bo'njoku, our arranged rendezvous point. We must have been an unusual sight as some thirty people were waiting on the bank to watch us come in. A well-built German called Uli, the World Wide Fund for Nature co-ordinator in the region, stood out from the crowd. Given the remoteness of our location and the difficulties of communication we were far from convinced that our arrangements would work out — someone had told us, 'The only thing that works properly in CAR are the termites' — but Uli was a man who made things happen. Within five minutes we had transferred to two sturdy Toyotas and were on our way.

We drove in convoy down a track of red earth through large pools of water, sending clouds of butterflies into the air. They were settled on the road for kilometre after kilometre, drinking in salts from the water. In the Dzanga-Sangha region alone, there are 316 species — we saw thousands of orange ones with a beautiful pinkish sheen, others that were dusty brown with pale mauve on the upper wing, and white ones, blue, black, yellow, and scarlet ones, that created a nebulous, fluttering kaleidoscope of colour all around us.

When we reached the police post there were butterflies densely clustered in patches on the ground, like luxurious rags strewn across the red earth. The first place we went into was what we thought was immigration. A substantial man in a blue kaftan sat behind a desk in a small room with a CB radio crackling in the corner. He greeted us all pleasantly, and we all settled down to a very long silent vigil as he meticulously copied out our filming permit, a two-page letter, into an old exercise book. Finally he carefully closed the exercise book, scribbled something onto the back of the original and then with great aplomb reached for his inkpad and stamped it. I got the impression he didn't get to do much paperwork tucked away in Lidjombo, and that he relished every moment.

Next we went in search of the local police. Once again, we were greeted enthusiastically by a policeman dressed in mix-and-match uniform and civilian clothes that seemed to suggest he was only half on duty. This didn't bode well for getting the kit through CAR customs quickly; we were fully expecting problems as six weeks earlier there had been a coup d'etat in CAR and the president had been overthrown. Still, as far as we could tell no one in the country seemed to mind much — they were pretty used to coups around here.

Whatever the political situation, it was clear that the authorities had got word of our arrival and moments later the local police commissionaire showed up. There was hand-shaking all round, and then we sat down in a row on a long wooden bench outside the building and watched pippit-like birds trying unsuccessfully to catch butterflies, while Uli went inside the small building to chat with him. After about five minutes an old pick-up drove up to us, its dashboard decorated in lurid pink, yellow and blue plastic flowers. It turned out to be the Mayor of Bayanga, the nearest town. He greeted us warmly and offered us his vehicle if we needed it. I was rather sorry that we didn't. We began to suspect some careful choreography when only minutes later an even more important official arrived — the Sous-prefet, or Deputy Administrator for the region, who easily outshone everyone else in his pink safari suit. He greeted Uli like a long lost friend and shook all our hands vigorously, promising us that CAR was safe, asking us to enjoy the country and telling us not to hesitate to contact him if there was anything we needed help with. We were all set.

About half an hour later we stopped at a Ba'aka village called Yandoumbe, a neat semi-circle of small huts, many of which were constructed from frames of interwoven saplings covered by a shaggy coat of dry leaves. This was

195

the home of Louis Sarno, the American anthropologist. He had no phone but had heard we were coming to CAR through the 'bush telegraph': messages are passed over the radio between various camps in Congo, CAR and Cameroon, then carried by word of mouth to others. He appeared from one of the larger huts, stooping through the low door. He was very tall and slender, towering over the Pygmies and deeply tanned, although he didn't look well. 'I've got malaria,' he explained, in a still-strong New Jersey accent. Despite this we spent the afternoon with him, discussing the problems facing the Ba'aka and their way of life. The south-western region of CAR contains the country's last large extent of primary forest, but even here the logging companies have made inroads. Most of the forest was logged in 1981 and was soon to be logged again.

Fortunately, with the WWF, the CAR government has set aside a reserve where the Ba'aka are allowed to hunt small antelope and monkeys. At the very heart of the reserve is a small area of true primary forest, where no hunting is permitted. This is where we were headed.

We stayed overnight in Bayanga and the following day bumped and rattled along the road into the forest. The deeper we went in, the more magnificent the trees became, the base of their trunks spreading out like buttresses of a Gothic cathedral. Once, a couple of red river hogs ran across the road.

I was sharing the back of a pick-up with Si and

Nigel. 'This is one of my all-time favourite things,' I said, 'driving through the African bush in the back of a pick-up.' It is the prospect of adventure I love, the not knowing what you might find round the next corner. On this road, though, it was all too predictable: a deep pool of muddy water. Our driver gunned the engine, we sped forward and got stuck. We leapt out of the back onto dry land while the driver revved the engine, the wheels spinning and spraying arcs of red mud into the air. Within minutes the sweat bees were on to us, buzzing in our faces and flying into our eyes. We were only a few kilometres from our destination, so we headed off on foot, leaving the driver with a couple of other guys to argue about whether or not the 4 × 4 diff locks had been engaged. 'Not' turned out to be the correct answer.

At Bai Hoku camp we met up with Chloe, an Italian biologist who has been following and studying a group of western lowland gorillas for the past five years. It takes several years to gain the trust of apes, and the gorillas were still very shy. To have a chance of seeing them we had to keep our numbers to the minimum, so only Si, Nigel and I accompanied Chloe and her Ba'aka tracker to find them. We walked briskly but quietly through the forest, and after about twenty-five minutes, Chloe whispered, 'We are close now, be very quiet and stick together.' She moved on, more slowly now, periodically clicking her tongue. 'I'm letting them know we're coming so as not to surprise them,' she murmured. A moment later we stopped. A young male gorilla was sitting on a fallen log directly in front of us. He contemplated us with mild curiosity, then disappeared into the undergrowth.

'Wow' I grinned at Chloe after he'd gone. She was grinning too — an encounter that close is rare.

We heard a soft grunt, a short sound followed by a longer sigh-like sound called a 'double grunt'. This is the most common of all gorilla calls and is used to keep in touch with other members of the group in the thick vegetation. Chloe gave a couple more clicks with her tongue and we moved forward slowly until her tracker stopped and pointed into the undergrowth. Chloe signalled for us to sit down on the ground, forming a tight group to appear as unthreatening as possible. Through thick vegetation we glimpsed another gorilla asleep on the ground about ten metres away, a large black shape in the shadows. It was late morning by now and a time when adult gorillas, having had a prolonged breakfast of fruit and herbaceous plants, take a siesta. Normally youngsters use this down-time to wrestle and play games such as 'King of the castle' or 'Follow my leader' but when we spotted the young male again he was quietly pulling away clay that plastered the base of a nearby tree. 'It's a shame, he's the only juvenile in the group so he hasn't got anyone to play with,' Chloe told us. I peered at him with my binoculars. He carefully peeled off lumps of clay and then hurriedly brought them up to his lips and nibbled the termites that scurried around in pandemonium inside.

After he finished his snack he wandered over to the reclining figure of his mother. At his approach she sat up and started to groom him. Adult gorillas rarely groom each other: social grooming is not as common as it is among chimps. Western lowland gorillas live in family groups with one silverback, a fully adult male, and anything from one to five females. Occasionally the silverback will groom one of his females or offspring but usually grooming occurs between a mother and her infants.

The young male was probably about six years old and still had a few more years before he left the group. While females may remain in their natal group, most young males leave at the age of about ten and wander alone, sometimes for years, until they acquire females from other groups and establish their own harem.

Thanks to the work of Diane Fossey in the Virunga National Park in Rwanda and other researchers we know a fair amount about mountain gorillas, but still very little is known about western and eastern lowland gorillas that live in the tropical rainforests of central and west Africa. The best estimate available is that there are about thirteen thousand lowland gorillas surviving in the wild today, but far too little of their range has been surveyed to be sure.

Recently, tragedy struck one of the best-known field sites in Congo, where several groups of gorillas had been followed and observed by the primatologist Magdalena Bermejo. In January 2003 an ebola epidemic struck in the region Cuvette-Ouest, killing a hundred people and 750 gorillas, two-thirds of the gorilla population in Lossi Park. Ebola is a virus that is passed on by infected body fluids and kills 90 per cent of its victims. It could easily spread into northern Congo and nearby Gabon, threatening thousands of people and more than 20,000 gorillas. It might prove to be the final nail in the coffin for western lowland gorillas. It is estimated that 30,000 remain and, given that there is already immense pressure on them from forest clearance and poaching, such an epidemic could send them to the brink of extinction. I asked Chloe if the disease might reach CAR.

'It is spreading north but it hasn't got anywhere near us yet — let's pray it stays that way,' she said.

Through the thick understorey we spied a patch of red-dish hair on the back of a huge, dome-shaped head. This was the boss, the silverback male himself. When he moved a metre or two, more of him became visible. He was nearly two metres at the shoulder and probably weighed over 200 kilos. 'He's called Mlima,' Chloe whispered. It was a good name: *Mlima* means 'mountain' in Swahili.

Then, suddenly, he charged, roaring as he ripped through the undergrowth towards us. He held his head high as he ran and his massive arms pounded the ground in front of him. At the last minute he veered off to one side, then stopped and glared at us, his arms held straight, resting on his knuckles. We stayed low and looked down at our shoelaces. Mlima charged again, but this time away from us and without roaring. He was just letting us know that he was the boss. It was his job to protect his family and he was doing it properly.

9

The Forest's Keepers

Andrea Turkalo knows her forest elephants. She has been studying them for thirteen years at Dzanga *bai* in the Central African Republic. She has identified over 3,000 individuals and knows several hundred well, one of which is LB. There is no doubt that she loves elephants, but some she loves more than others, and LB belongs in the latter category. The first night in her camp Andrea told us of her trials with LB.

'LB?' we asked.

'Little Bastard,' she said. 'A young bull elephant who sometimes wanders into camp at night and causes havoc.' Andrea had spent more than one night defending the kitchen, sitting up with a torch and banging pots and pans together to deter him from bursting in. 'He isn't that bothered, though, he backs off a bit and sways about, pretending he's going to charge. Anyway, I've got a door on the kitchen now so, hopefully, that'll stop him visiting.'

Her confident tone didn't prevent us from having a rather fitful night, waking at the slightest sound and imagining in our sleepy minds elephants peering down at us in our beds.

Dzanga *bai* is a huge clearing in the forest where elephants and other animals congregate. It takes about forty minutes to get there from Andrea's camp, but you have to wade up a muddy stream that turns sandy and, on the last stretch, is full of elephant dung. It is too deep for wellingtons, so we rolled up our trousers and went barefoot. At first we had tried wearing sandals but Andrea and her Ba'aka trackers didn't, and we soon discovered why. It's a darned sight better walking through elephant dung barefoot than having it stick between your sandals and the soles of your feet. Also, you don't have to spend the rest of the day in footwear encrusted with dried elephant dung. The outward journey from camp in the morning, when the air was still relatively cool, was considerably more pleasant than the return, when the sun had been warming the shallow pools: walking barefoot through warm, pungent elephant dung was an experience I could have lived without.

Once out of the stream we followed a well-demarcated trail. It was the kind of small, meandering path you might find in a forest or woodland anywhere, unremarkable in every way but one: it was not man-made. On either side the bark at head height on many trees had been worn smooth and shiny by decades of rubbing, which gave a strong clue as to the origin of the trails. Also, every now and again we came across enormous, deep round imprints in the muddy ground and large piles of dung. We were on a trail made by elephants, and one which appeared to be used regularly.

Throughout this region of the Congo Basin elephants have been heavily poached so they tend to be nervous of people and steer clear of them. However, if you come across one unexpectedly in the forest, it may well charge. And, if you don't get out of the way in time, you will probably be killed, speared on its tusks, thrown around like a rag doll, then trampled into the ground. Some have lived to tell the tale, but they have impressive scars to go with their stories. There are an estimated 200,000 elephants left in the Congo Basin, but their distribution is patchy. We were in an area with one of the highest elephant densities, an estimated one per square kilometre.

'So, what happens if we meet one?' Nigel asked.

'Well, mostly they run away,' Andrea said, 'but sometimes they charge, in which case you run.'

You might think you would hear such a large animal moving through the bushes, but elephants can be amazingly quiet. Even in thick under-growth they may be very close, within metres, without your realising. What usually gives them away is their smell: a strong, musky odour somewhat reminiscent of horse manure.

Banda, one of the trackers who worked with Andrea, led the way. He was short and muscular, with a shaven head and, like many of the Ba'aka, his teeth were filed into sharp points. He would have looked intimidating, had it not been for his lively eyes and broad smile. At one stage he stopped abruptly and peered into the vegetation. In the undergrowth there was a movement followed by a sound like a short exhalation of breath. '*Njoku*,' he whispered. Elephant. A few metres off the path I glimpsed a large shape, denser and darker than the surrounding shadows. A branch waved at head height and then there was silence. The elephant had not wanted to meet us and had slipped away.

As we progressed towards Dzanga *bai* we came across several junctions. Narrow paths led off the main route, winding into the forest, and frequently we came to a fork or a major crossroads. I couldn't help wondering where they all went. Researchers following similar trails have found that they go on and on, connecting to others, so that ultimately the whole Congo Basin is criss-crossed by a network of elephant paths covering hundreds of kilometres of jungle.

Singly or in small groups elephants might have relatively little impact, but the traffic along these paths had been enough to wear them smooth. They might have been in use for generations, hundreds, perhaps even thousands, of years.

Countless elephant feet over countless generations have landscaped the forests of Central Africa.

The antiquity of the paths is suggested by the mature trees, such as Autrenella, Annonidium, Duboscia and Omphalocarpum, that line them — favourite food trees that were probably planted by the ancestors of today's herds. Elephants are not only the landscapers here, they are also the gardeners of the forest.

The diet of forest elephants includes a significant amount of fruit, and lots of different seeds are found in their dung: on average they drop a phenomenal 45 kilos every day. In a forest environment, where every bit of nutrient is valuable, each pile acts like a gro-bag. The seeds pass through the elephant's gut and are deposited on the ground in a nutritious heap of fertiliser. Studies have shown that 96 per cent of all elephant dung piles contain seedlings, which are not only given a head start by the elephant compost but are planted in the best possible position: on the paths, which are more open and provide the seedlings with light.

Elephants are exceptional as seed dispersers, and not only because of the quantity they consume, the fertiliser and light they provide, but because they disperse seeds over such a wide area. Along with gorillas and chimpanzees, who are also big fruit-eaters, they are principally responsible for dispersing at least thirty different species of tree. Species such as Autrenella and Omphalocarpum rely exclusively on elephants to plant their seeds.

While many plants and animals rely closely on each other in forests, some species such as elephants, chimpanzees and gorillas are called 'keystone' species because they play a pivotal role in maintaining the forest ecosystem. Their disappearance from a habitat is likely to trigger the loss of other resident species, which in turn prompts the loss of yet more species, connections unravel and a disastrous domino effect ensues.

We continued along the track until we came to a place where the ground was worn hard and clear of low vegetation in a circular area around an Omphalocarpum tree. Several trails radiated out, leading to and from it like a roundabout in a busy city centre. It was obvious that when the tree was in fruit, as it was then, it attracted pretty heavy elephant traffic. The fruit of the Omphalocarpum is a monstrous-looking thing; also known as the belly-button fruit, it is nearly the size of a football, rotund but slightly flattened with a deep dimple on one side. It grows directly on the tree-trunk. I picked up a fruit that had fallen to the ground and was amazed at how heavy it was — a couple of kilos at least. It was also rock hard and smelt faintly of garlic. It didn't look especially appetising to me, but elephants love it.

Out on the plains, savannah elephants subsist mainly on bark and leaves. In the forest their diet is more varied, with many fruits, seeds and roots and so they are equipped with downward-pointing tusks that are ideal for spearing and splitting open fallen fruits, such as Omphalocarpum. Forest elephants also tend to go about in much smaller groups because food is more sporadic here than it is in the savannah, and harder to find. Moreover, in the rainforest the fruiting patterns of many trees are far less regular than in temperate forests. But the Omphalocarpum makes sure that the elephants know it is open season: the gigantic fruit makes a loud, distinctive thud when it hits the ground, alerting all the elephants in the area. But, like chimpanzees and gorillas, the elephants almost certainly have a detailed mental map of the forest, which pinpoints key trees, and as well as specialist knowledge that enables them to predict when particular trees will be in fruit.

The well-worn roundabout around the Omphalocarpum emphasized how important a single tree can be. Elephants had obviously been coming here for decades at least, knowledge of its location and fruiting patterns passed down from mothers to their offspring. Andrea told us that she had seen a particular male in the same area on precisely the same day for several years running. But while we know that elephants' movements are not random, we still know little about where and how far they travel.

In Bomassa we had met a scientist called Steve Blake, who was studying the movements of elephants. He had spent three weeks in the forest trying, with the help of his wife and a vet, to dart elephants and fit radio collars on them. They had hoped to fit twenty-eight collars in three weeks, but when we had seen them they had managed to dart only one elephant. On their second to last day Steve was getting desperate. Later, they returned unsuccessful again and, in Steve's case, lacerated by thorns.

'What happened?' I asked.

'We found a big male but he was in quite dense vegetation. That's really tough because then you have to get very close — you can't really use the dart gun, you almost have to sneak up and stick the needle straight into the elephant's backside. It is pretty dangerous because even if you succeed the tranquilliser doesn't take effect immediately and you're likely to find yourself next to an angry elephant rampaging about in the bush. Anyway, we got very close to him and were just sneaking up to where we could fire a dart when he caught wind of us and charged — I ran and fell into a thorny bush, as you can see.' He looked down ruefully at his blood-stained shins. 'It's really disappointing, though, because we only have limited time and money. But having said that I'd rather we failed than anyone or an elephant got hurt.'

Later we heard that on their last day they darted another elephant. This dangerous and difficult work is invaluable in deepening our understanding of how forest elephants live and journey through the forests of the Congo basin. Steve has discovered from elephants he has radio-collared in the past that they can travel as far as 60 kilometres a day. One elephant walked 105 kilometres in a straight line over a couple of days. Obviously he knew exactly where he was going — perhaps to an Omphalocarpum tree his mother had shown him, or perhaps to an even more important destination like the one we were heading for.

As we continued along the elephant trail, there were more junctions and the path got wider as others joined it, until finally it turned into a wide sandy boulevard, flanked by tall trees. All of a sudden we emerged from the forest into a huge open clearing. It was an area about half a kilometre long and a quarter wide, the equivalent of about twenty football pitches, traversed by a small stream. In the middle of the glade there were patches of bare ground, muddy puddles and deep holes; beyond, marshy ground was covered with pea-green sedges. Ironwood or Mokole trees were scattered around the perimeter, their young orangy-pink leaves forming fiery bouquets in the late-afternoon light.

We felt a sense of jubilation on coming out into the open after the closeness of the forest, but the sight that greeted us was simply astonishing. It felt a bit like stumbling across the Garden of Eden. Scores of elephants wandered about, mingling with elegant antelopes such as sitatunga, duiker and the shy but beautiful striped bongo. There were dark-coloured giant forest hogs, and russet red river hogs, displaying fancy ear tassels. A herd of pretty forest buffalo were lazing in the mud, and there was a multitude of wading birds, egrets, hammerkops, ducks. It was a wonderful window on the forest, a place where animals came out from the trees and gathered together in peace and tranquillity.

No sooner had I thought this than a young

male elephant ran towards a lone buffalo and chased it to the edge of the clearing. This startled a family of sitatunga and pandemonium spread. Several elephants stampeded to the far corner of the clearing, their trunks waving in the air and their ample bottoms swaying behind them. But everything settled down again as quickly as it had started — it was just young blood having a bit of fun.

We had climbed up on to a viewing platform, a mirador, from where the whole clearing was spread out below us. It is probably the only place in the world where forest elephants can be observed directly and information gathered on their population dynamics and social behaviour.

Andrea settled down, notebook in hand, to record their comings and goings and interactions. 'That's Myrtle,' she said, indicating a medium-sized female with a distinctive neat round hole in her left ear. 'And over there is Vicky, and her family. That's Tess . . . And that large bull is Dennis. Those two young females are Elvira One and Two. They're sisters, Elvira One is seven years old and Elvira Two is three. They've had a hard time as their mother was killed last year.'

I looked at Elvira One, a pretty young female who was covered in bright red mud. Her head was down and her trunk submerged in the water. The reason why elephants come here in such numbers to get mineral salts and clay rather than food and drink.

This clearing was the *bai*, a word that comes

from the Ba'aka language and means 'the place where the animals eat'. They are an extraordinary feature of the Central African rainforest, often found in low-lying areas where the water-table is high, making it difficult for trees to grow. Their locations are also frequently linked to the presence of intrusions of a rock called dolerite in the granite soil. The clearings may be small or large, but they play a vital role in the lives of forest animals.

Large mammals are attracted to *bais* because they are rich in minerals, such as sodium, potassium, calcium, magnesium, phosphorus and manganese. Without them large herbivores would have nothing to overcome mineral deficiencies and imbalances, while the clay is probably important in helping to neutralise the plant toxins. But Dzanga *bai* must be exceptional, as no other clearing is known to attract such large numbers of elephants and other animals.

We watched the elephants digging deep holes, to reach rich seams of minerals. Sometimes they occur on dry land, but more often it seems they are under the streams. The holes fill with water, but the elephants return time and again to the same ones, perhaps picking them out by smell even though they are under water. They reach deep into the holes with their trunks and blow noisy bubbles, which stirs up the water and creates a rich soup of minerals, which they suck up and pour into their mouths, relishing it as though it was a fine wine.

The scene was as colourful as it was noisy. The elephants were all painted with different-coloured mud — some had neat red booties, others had yellow knees, trunks and faces from where they'd knelt down to drink, some were almost entirely white where they'd wallowed in muddy pools and others were just shiny black and wet. We could identify exactly which mud-hole they'd visited recently, and which other elephants they'd been hanging out with because they were similarly anointed. Mothers and their calves tended to have perfectly matching patterns, but where the mothers might be wearing red ankle socks their calves had on thigh-length boots.

I wondered if these embellishments made the elephants more difficult for Andrea to recognise, but she wasn't easily fooled. 'One day Elvira found a microphone we had planted in one of the holes to get some good recordings of them blowing. She pulled it out and destroyed it. It might be my imagination, but she looked a little guilty afterwards and wandered off. Later she returned wearing a mask of yellow mud, but I knew exactly who she was.'

Spread out below us some eighty elephants were taking their salts and socialising. Individuals and family groups arrived along paths from all different directions, the adolescents usually hurrying ahead of the rest. Deep guttural rumbles travelled the length of the *bai* as friends and relatives greeted each other. Out in the water, calves complained loudly when their mothers pushed them away from a good hole, while the males followed strict protocol to avoid major disputes.

At one end of the *bai* there was a dry area that resembled a construction site. On a large mound of earth next to a deep crater a sub-adult male was waiting his turn to dig. Below him, Dennis was expanding the hole, kicking at the earth with his front leg, then scooping up loose dirt with his trunk and depositing it in his mouth. He had been there for nearly an hour and seemed in no hurry to move on. The sub-adult continued to wait patiently. A younger male arrived to take his place in the queue. A bit optimistic, I thought. Sure enough, an hour later the youngster had wandered off but the sub-adult was still waiting; he had moved a few paces round and stood with one black leg crossed against the other and his trunk draped over a tusk, the picture of resigned boredom.

Elephants do not create this landscape of *bais*, but they do transform it. They shape the contours of the *bais*, develop and maintain them. And through their labours they make minerals available to other large herbivores, such as bongo and buffalo, who also need them and would not otherwise be able to get to them. The streams and pools become rich in dissolved salts as minerals are pumped up from the ground below the water. Further access to minerals is created at the periphery of the *bai*, where the elephants, excavating clay and minerals, have dug caves into the ground reaching depths of 10 metres.

Hundreds of *bais* are scattered through the Central African rainforest, some small, others

214

huge, but each with its own unique mix of animals. The *bai* near Mbeli in the Congo was almost a swamp, full of lush herbaceous plants, aquatic herbs and water-lilies. Elephants visited it, but it was especially frequented by gorillas. We had been there one afternoon and spied a lone silverback called Isaac eating water-lilies on the far side. Or rather I should say we watched the back of his head, as he sat obscured on a tufted island of sedges and ate water lilies.

Gorillas can spend hours munching steadfastly and for them the Mbeli *bai* was like a massive salad bowl. When they eat water lilies, gorillas consume the whole plant but they do it methodically: first the leaves, then the stem, then the root ball. Before they begin, a little preparation is required. The plant is pulled out of the mud and carefully washed. Youngsters try to copy the adults, but the lilies are often quite stubborn. They pull and pull, and when they finally rip out a plant they fall over backwards. Then, imitating the adults without really knowing what they're supposed to be doing, they wave the plant in the general direction of the water and proceed to eat it, still muddy, usually managing the stem and leaves before being defeated by the tough root.

One day while the film crew made their way to the mirador in Dzanga *bai*, Andrea, Matofi, one of the Ba'aka trackers, and I skirted our way round to the south end of the clearing. We avoided the main elephant paths as much as possible — this was one of the principal directions from which elephants entered the *bai*

215

and we weren't keen to meet a group wandering through the forest. It was late morning, a compromise between coming early, when there weren't too many elephants around, and later, when the *bai* would look its best for filming. As we got closer to our destination the elephant paths crossed more frequently and there were a number of quite open areas where the vegetation had been flattened. Finally a Spaghetti Junction of paths resolved itself into a highway that led into the *bai*. We peered both ways and, on seeing that the coast was clear, stepped out into the open.

I called the mirador on my walkie-talkie to let them know we were in position. The plan was that Si would film me from there as I came out into the clearing and did a piece to camera about the nature of *bais* and their importance to forest animals. Andrea and Matofi chose a stout tree to hide behind so as not to be in shot while I continued into the *bai*. Some buffalo in their wallowing baths eyed me suspiciously. Unlike elephants, buffalo have good eyesight and they clocked me the moment I arrived. On the other hand elephants have an exceptionally acute sense of smell and a few were over on the far side of the *bai*, but I was downwind of them and thought I could creep out without being rumbled. Unfortunately, they were in the wrong place for our shot, so when I'd got about a hundred metres out I sat down and waited.

About twenty minutes later a sub-adult male elephant appeared on the edge of the forest to my left. He was some distance away, cautiously sniffing the air with his trunk. I stayed absolutely still and hoped he wouldn't notice me. After another ten minutes he came out, walked past where I sat, some hundred metres away, and wandered into the *bai*. We continued to wait. Every now and then I'd scan the trees around me. Andrea and Matofi were watching my back, but I felt they might be a bit far off to give me a quiet 'Psst' if an elephant came strolling down the boulevard behind me. I didn't want any last-minute surprises.

We waited a little longer. It was close to midday when the *bai* would get busier. I was just wondering whether I'd hear an elephant coming up behind me when I looked over my left shoulder and saw a statuesque female with curving white tusks and a small calf at her side. They were less than ten metres away and heading in my direction. So far they hadn't seen me, but my heart was beating fast. I froze as the big female kept coming towards me. Then she changed course a fraction. I prayed she would pass diagonally in front of me . . . hopefully without ever knowing I was there.

I had a radio microphone clipped to my shirt so that I could talk to Jake without having to use the walkie-talkie. 'I'm going to do the piece now, okay?' I whispered to my collar.

As the walkie-talkie crackled into life with the reply, the elephant turned her head towards me searching the air with her trunk.

'No, I'll cue you with the walkie-talkie, Charlotte, just hold it a second or two more until she comes right into frame.'

Just what size is the frame? I thought nervously. I felt horribly vulnerable, sitting on my own, right out in the open. A moment later the walkie-talkie bleeped, giving me my cue. I introduced the *bai* — succinctly — looking towards the camera, which I could no longer see as the elephant was now directly in front of me. At the sound of the radio and my voice she turned and took a few paces towards me, rocking her head from side to side and flapping her ears. I got up and started walking back towards the tree trying to move smoothly. Then, out of the corner of my eye, I saw her charge.

A tank of grey, she came fast, trunk tucked under, ears spread wide and tusks like spears pointing straight at me. It is amazing how small and flimsy you feel when faced with 2000 kilos of elephant hurtling at you. In a matter of seconds my nervousness had turned to fear and then into the certainty that I was about to die. I ran for all I was worth, bounded up a small bank without breaking pace and sped towards the tree where Andrea and Matofi had been waiting. They had leapt out from behind it and were shouting at the elephant for all they were worth. She hesitated. I was now only a few metres from the tree and thought I might make it. But then she charged again at point-blank range.

I remember feeling surprised as much as anything else by what was happening, and oddly detached too. Fortunately instinct took over. I spun round to face the elephant, pumped up by a surge of adrenaline. I grabbed a stout log from the ground and hurled it at her, screaming. Again, she hesitated, standing only a couple of metres from me, bellowing and shaking her head, her trunk swaying from side to side. She backed away a pace or two, then came forward again, as though preparing to charge once more. Still shouting, the three of us leapt behind the tree and mentally braced ourselves for the impact.

The tree was large enough for us all to cower behind, but with a girth of over five metres and a smooth, straight trunk all the way up to the canopy we wouldn't have had a hope of climbing it even if we'd been gibbons. A quick scan of our surroundings left us in no doubt that there was nowhere we could run to if she came for us. I was drenched in sweat, and blood was pumping in my eardrums. Thankfully, she decided that finding her calf, who had run off into the bush when the furore started, was a higher priority than skewering us.

'It's Samantha,' Andrea whispered, as the elephant's backside disappeared into the foliage. 'She's really angry. I'm so sorry I didn't warn you, but she came out into the bai where she was obscured by this tree and by the time we saw her she was right on you. I thought you'd had it.'

I was limp with fear now. Andrea and Matofi looked shaken too. 'Is she going to come back?' I whispered. 'And what do we do if she does?'

'Let's just be very still and hope she calms down,' Andrea replied, then exchanged some whispered words with Matofi.

'My God, she's big — that was scary, I just

can't believe — ' Words tumbled out of me.

'We should be very quiet,' Andrea murmured. 'She's still just in there.' She gestured over my head to the clump of trees from which Samantha had first emerged just a few — long — minutes before. I saw some branches move.

'Bl-eee-p,' went the walkie-talkie, which now was no longer on my belt but lying on the open ground somewhere between us and the spot where I'd been sitting in the *bai*. Nigel's concerned voice floated over to us: 'Are you okay?'

There was a movement in the bushes.

'Ssh,' whispered Andrea. 'Tell them not to use the radio, she's still very close. She might come back. She charged twice — she really meant it.'

Fortunately I was still wired with my radio microphone and whispered, 'Jake, please don't use the radio. She's still very close, the noise is freaking her out. I've dropped my walkie-talkie somewhere out there and can't get to it.'

Gradually our fear subsided. We kept checking out possible escape routes, but after about half an hour it appeared that Samantha had decided against killing us.

It was now well after midday and more and more elephants would come into the *bai*. It was time to leave if we didn't want any more excitement. We decided against going through the forest, with the risk of bumping into any more elephants, especially as Samantha, whom Matofi could still see, was now a bit further into the bushes with her calf, nursing her grievances. Instead we would go boldly across the *bai*. We broke cover and moved forward cautiously, looking over our shoulders and expecting Samantha to hurtle out at us.

'Can we outrun her if she comes for us?' I asked.

'Yes, over a short distance, if we cross on fairly firm ground.'

Our shoes squelched into deep mud, but with each pace we felt better. The *bai* had emptied of elephants during the commotion, but a herd of buffalo remained at the far end. They started to move towards us, then broke into a canter, veering away and back again as they navigated the ground between the channels of water. When we were about two-thirds of the way across they passed us on the right, then turned and stopped dead, staring at us intently. A couple of cocky characters blustered forwards, and a few more stepped up behind them, backing them up. I had just had an adrenalin hit that would last me for a decade and was in no mood for confrontation with a herd of buffalo. I glowered at them. At any other time I might have been nervous about having a staring match with them, but now they seemed comical. I imagined them as a Gary Larson cartoon, saying to each other, 'You go first.' 'No, after you.' Andrea and I shouted at them in unison, 'Get lost. *Shoo*,' and they stopped.

Moments later we were climbing the ladder to the mirador and being greeted warmly by the crew.

'Jake, that was your big chance to save the day *and* . . . ?' I said hands on hip. I was joking, of course — there was nothing that anyone could have done and he had sort of saved the day by getting the walkie-talkie switched off.

Later I reflected on my near miss. You never know in advance how you might react to a situation like that. Deep down I had always suspected that if an elephant charged me I would run, which of course was exactly what I had done, but secretly I was pleased to know that my fight response had come into play: when I couldn't outrun Samantha I had turned to face her — and I had been angry. If she'd kept coming I would have fought her with every ounce of my strength, which was somehow quite comforting. I also wondered whether the whole incident could have been avoided if I had stayed stock still after doing my piece to camera rather than getting up and walking away. Perhaps she would have stopped and continued into the *bai* — or charged. Had it been the latter it would have been too late to run. I simply couldn't have risked it. As for Samantha, I bore her no grudge: she was only going about her business and it must have been a mighty unpleasant shock to encounter me. I'm glad she doesn't trust humans.

Two nights later, at about three a.m., we heard a gunshot ring out in the forest. The next day I asked Andrea about it and she thought someone had probably been after antelope. But a couple of days later it happened again. We had been out in a different part of the forest and came back to find her distressed. Several shots had been fired in succession, she told us, and then several more, suggesting that an elephant had been killed this time. James and Jake had been at the *bai* and had also heard the shots. They reported that the elephants had been quietly taking minerals but had suddenly gone crazy. Within minutes the place had been deserted.

Andrea told us that she had had word that morning, through a Ba'aka friend, that one of the most notorious elephant poachers was in the forest. She had tried desperately to contact the authorities by radio but had had no response. An anti-poaching patrol was stationed nearby and when Andrea met up with them they told her that they had heard the shots and gone out to investigate but couldn't find any sign of anyone. She insisted that they go back and look again, but they soon returned: they had been prevented from passing through the forest by marauding elephants.

That evening we heard the cries of a lost calf. It was a heart-rending sound and I prayed that it had only been separated from its mother during the chaos of the day and that she had not been killed. Whatever the case, it was not only this youngster that was upset: disquiet had spread, and throughout the night the calls of agitated elephants echoed round the forest.

What was happening? We were in a national park with a strong research presence, a developing tourist interest and the support of the WWF — it is one of the best protected areas in Central Africa — yet poachers could kill an elephant within earshot of Andrea's camp. And it was not a one-off. Only a week before, the anti-poaching patrol had found the carcass of a young male. It had been mortally wounded, but must still have managed to run sufficiently far from its killers that they lost it and were unable to recover its ivory.

Andrea's long-term data showed a frightening trend: there were fewer and fewer mature animals in the population. Youngsters without families, such as the Elviras, are common, but young calves seldom survive long without their mothers. 'An elephant doesn't even have to have big tusks for them to kill it. They'll shoot whatever they come across. It is easy enough to do and they can sell the meat as well as the ivory.'

Combating poaching in Central Africa is far from easy. A good collaboration has been developed between the Congo, Cameroon and the Central African Republic in terms of tracking down and prosecuting poachers, but in a region with so many wars there is no shortage of guns. Moreover, these countries have many desperate social problems that stem from extreme poverty and political instability so it is unsurprising that elephant protection is low on their list of priorities.

Soon after we left the Central African Republic we heard from Andrea that another elephant had been killed in Dzanga.

It is not only elephants that are threatened by poaching but a host of other animals including the great apes. In the last few years poaching in Central and West Africa has reached staggering levels; the vast majority of slaughtered animals go to supply the rapidly burgeoning trade in 'bushmeat'.

Hunting wild animals for food has always been practised by small, remote forest communities, but in the last decade or so it has changed in character. Now it is big business: 5 million tonnes of wild-animal meat is taken out of the forest each year to feed the populations of the growing forest towns and cities, and line the pockets of businessmen.

The principal reason for this is that logging companies have opened up vast tracts of forest with roads and attracted large numbers of people, who are looking for employment, into the forest. More often than not, when the logging operation moves to a new area they leave their labour force behind as it is easier and cheaper to recruit new workers at the next location. This means people are left with no jobs but easy access to the forest, so many have turned to hunting and selling bushmeat as a means to earn their living. Now businessmen are encouraging hunting on an unprecedented scale. If the trade continues as it is, many species will be soon eradicated from the forests of Central Africa.

A month or so earlier, we had spent a few days in Yaounde, the capital of Cameroon, filming orphan gorillas and chimpanzees rescued after poachers had killed their mothers. Once a week a train comes into Yaounde piled with the carcasses of duikers and monkeys, chimpanzees and gorillas. It is illegal to hunt many of these animals, but no one seems to care.

We met an Israeli colonel who had moved to Cameroon about seven years ago with an Israeli mission to train special forces. He had remained at the personal request of President Biya, to advise on the training and deployment of the presidential guard and special forces. It was unusual to meet a man in his position, and even more so for such a man to harbour a deep concern for wildlife.

With his military background the colonel had an interesting take on the bushmeat problem. Many conservation efforts are directed at protecting forests and introducing anti-poaching patrols, but he thought it would be best to tackle the poachers directly. Over dinner he told us, 'There are probably three hundred serious commercial hunters in Cameroon. If you ask them why they hunt, they say it makes them a good living. But it's still only about a hundred dollars a month. If you could pay them the same to become rangers instead, I'm sure they would agree. It would only cost thirty thousand dollars a month. It's usually the chiefs in the villages who own the guns anyway, and they wield huge influence. Get them on your side and they could have a massive impact on the bushmeat trade in Cameroon. Of course, checks and safeguards would have to be put in place, and even then some people would continue to poach, but the people eating the meat aren't wealthy. If chimpanzee meat is scarce and the price goes up, they would go back to eating chicken and goat.'

If you estimate that in other Central and West African countries combined there may be a thousand commercial poachers, it would cost a hundred thousand dollars a month to deploy them as rangers. It doesn't seem like a very high price to pay to prevent animals like chimpanzees and gorillas being eaten to extinction. The scheme would be most effective in tandem with the protection of forests, changes in attitudes to bushmeat, better gun control and changes in logging practices.

Forests are an important resource for many countries around the world, and local people and governments must be able to benefit from them. But the truth is that the profits go not to governments or local people but to the logging companies, their shareholders and retailers abroad. While in parts of the Amazon locals receive $30 US per tree, the timber from the same tree sells on the export market for upwards of $3,300 US. The same tree may then be made into dining tables with a total retail value of as much as $128,250. That's the equivalent of the revenue from 4,275 trees in the forest. In particular the practice of exporting raw wood rather than adding value by working it in the country of origin removes the profits from the hands that most need it.

And we are still blind to the real riches of the forest — the medicines and other products that could be harvested to the benefit of local people and wider humanity without damaging ecosystems. Would *you* rather have a dining-table or a cure for cancer?

The world's forests are now carved up into logging concessions dotted with little islands of precarious national parks. The rainforests' animals and trees are being plundered faster than ever. The rate of deforestation around the world is not declining as many people hope but is dramatically on the rise. Recent figures show that there has been a shocking 40% increase in logging in the Amazon since 1996. Data based on satellite observations reveal that between 2001 and 2002 an area the size of Belgium was burned or cut down. Much of this is not even for valuable timber but to grow soya beans that are exported to Europe as cheap cattle feed for intensively farmed animals. At current levels of logging, within twenty years there will be no substantial tracts of forest left.

As you walk between towering trees surrounded by an infinite variety of life, the rainforest appears to be Nature at her most robust. To some extent, given time, logged forests can be regenerated — but if too much is taken they are doomed. During my time in rainforests I have learnt that they are, above all, a tight-knit community, an intricate web of relationships between plants, animals and their environment. Remove too many keystone species or too many trees, and the whole system will collapse, leaving a dry, barren wasteland.

We all have a responsibility to try to turn the tide of destruction and in the western world we have the capability to do it. We do not have to buy furniture made from non-regenerating hardwoods. The loss of the rainforest has profound consequences for us all, influencing climate, rainfall patterns, and destroying the greatest bank of life on earth. For some it also means the loss of their home.

On our last day in the Central African Republic we spent the day in the forest with Louis Sarno and a group of Ba'aka women from Yandoumbe. They showed us how they make their homes in the forest. With everyone talking, joking and laughing they constructed a lattice framework of saplings and then split the stems of wide leaves to hook over the frame to cover it, creating a perfect green dome. After a while three of them went off to gather more leaves. As they walked they began to sing. Their voices were pure, powerful and lyrical, each voice layering on top of the others and intertwining to form harmonies of stunning complexity. The sounds seemed to have evolved from the natural environment, the notes floating up and down in the air, weaving through the branches of the trees as though the trees themselves were singing. While scientists strive to learn about the intricate connections between species in the rainforest, the Ba'aka seem to understand its soul.

I asked Louis to ask one of the women what they thought would happen if all the rainforest disappeared. She looked mystified, then laughed and assured me that the forest was very large and it would always be there. But when Louis pressed her and asked her what if it *is* all destroyed, she paused for a time and then replied, 'It cannot go, or there will be nothing left and we will all die in the sun.'

Acknowledgements

First I would like to express my warmest thanks to the whole team at the BBC Natural History Unit in Bristol with whom I made the series 'Jungle'. In particular, I would like to say what a pleasure it has been to work with Karen Bass, the series producer, Mark Flowers the producer of the Waterworld programme in the Amazon, who also was kind enough to do the lovely illustrations in the book, and to Scott Alexander who directed the Canopy programme in Thailand and Borneo and was very patient about my fear of heights. My thanks also to Nigel Pope, who directed the Underworld programme in the Congo and Central African Republic and shared many adventures. Mark Fox and Chris Mallett did a wonderful job of editing the programmes, Paul Cowgill produced an excellent sound track, Graham Wild, the dubbing editor, produced a great mix, while Sophie Cooper made many valuable additions to the commentary. I would like to also thank Sara Ford, the executive producer and Neil Nightingale the head of the NHU for their enthusiasm for the project and their valuable comments on the programmes. Rita Aspinall and Cristina Hughes our production co-ordinators were brilliant — Rita looked after us both in the office and on location in the Amazon and Borneo, and Cristina was a great help in sorting out photographs for the book.

Many thanks also to Sally Mark the production manager, to Lawrence Breen, a footage specialist and researchers Anna Mike and James Chapman. Above all I would like to express my sincerest thanks to assistant producer, Vicky Web and researcher, Jonnie Hughes, who not only did a great deal of research for the programmes but were also very helpful in conducting additional research for the book, liasing with scientists and checking facts and figures for me — in fact, it would have been impossible for me to write this book without them.

The subject of rain forest ecology is vast and so we were extremely fortunate to have as consultants many top scientists working in this field. I would like to especially thank Richard Corlett of the University of Hong Kong, Richard Primack of Boston University, Sir Ghillean Prance, Will Crampton of University of Florida, Pilai Poonswad of Mahidol University, Professor Francis Halle of the Laboratoire de Botanique Tropicale in Montpellier, France. Many other scientists also gave us the benefit of their expert knowledge Professor Patrick Culbert of University of Arizona, Nick Brown of the University of Oxford, Professor David Bignell of the University of London, Queen Mary, Bill Sellers of Loughborough University, Professor Nigel Franks and Professor Gareth Jones of the University of Bristol, Professor Richard Byrne of the University of St Andrews, Brian Spooner of the Royal Botanical Gardens at Kew, Mya Thompson of the Elephant Listening Project, Christian Thompson of WWF and Andrew

Mitchell of the Global Canopy Programme. Also to Professor Alan Feduccia of University of North Carolina, Dr Jeff Hall and Dr Margaret Kinnaird of the World Conservation Society, Dr Stephen Sutton, Dr Glen Reynolds of the Danum Valley Research Centre, Dr Nalini Nadkarni of the Smithsonian Tropical Research Institute, Dr Lisa Curran of the University of Michigan, Dr Martin Ellwood of Cambridge University and Maria Gracia — Co-ordinator of Pacaya Samiria Program and Co-ordinator of Ecotourism Pro Naturaleza.

It was a pleasure to work with camerman Si Wagen and sound recordist Jake Drake Brockman. Si and Jake are much more than talented professionals, they are great travelling companions and there are few people I would rather roam around the rainforests of the world with. I would like to also express my deepest gratitude to James Aldred and Andy Barrell for being so calm and reassuring and helping me get over my fear of heights in order to explore the canopy, as well as for the many interesting conversations we had while perched in the tree-tops.

On location in Sabah, we had the help of many excellent people including, Dany Cleyet-Marrel and Laurent Pyot, who brought the cinebulle and balloon to Borneo providing us with an amazing new perspective on the canopy, Cede Prudente our fixer, who also took many of the pictures in the book and Sylvia Yorath, a senior conservation officer at Danum. Thank you also to botanist Berndus Balaola, better known as 'Mike', for sharing his extraordinary knowledge of plants with me and to John Pike, who was especially helpful in answering my many queries about the forest in Danum Valley. My deepest thanks to Professor Birute Galdikas, Steven Brend and all the dedicated staff of the Orangutan Foundation at the orphanage in Pankalangbun in Kalimantan for being so kind and helpful to us when we visited. I am also very grateful to Melvin Gumal for his assistance in Sarawak and for graciously answering my barrage of questions about the future of the forest there. In Cambodia we were fortunate to have the assistance of Seng Lo, Major Ian Brookes, Dean Johnson and Sunny Chhoun, and in Thailand, Toswan Devakul, who was always thinking one step ahead. I would also like to thank Sara Bumrungsri, a bat scientist who showed me how to search for bats in the canopy with a bat detector, Toh, a wonderful field assistant and wildlife artist and Pea'ak and Jeb who deserve a special mention for their expert coffee-making skills.

Our journey to the Amazon was one of the most memorable trips I've ever made and I would like to say a special thank you to Roberto Lara, our fixer who shared his knowledge and enthusiasm for Peru with us and became a great friend. Thank you also to Pepe Lopez and the rafting team: Antonio, Kachimera, Leo and Piero for our adventures on the whitewater of the Kosnipata and Pilcopata rivers. I would also like to warmly thank Walter Mancilla, Salvatore and Guillermo Knell, Mario and Ramon for being such excellent guides and many thanks to Paul for hiring us the beautiful *Delfin* with which we were able to explore the Amazon River. Many thanks also to Saul Gutierrez for his help in Venezuela.

It was great to have the assistance of Wildlife Conservation Society in Congo and I would particularly like to thank Brian Curran and Mark Gately, the directors of the Bomassa Research Centre, for their logistical help and provision of cold beer. I am also grateful to Steve Blake for telling me about his fascinating research on elephants. We were very fortunate to have the help of Boo Maisels of WCS, who is a very good naturalist and whose evident love of the forest makes her a wonderful guide and a huge thank you also to Mosombo, Apumu, Manjele, Njiobese, Dogoli, Tuksma, Emili, Majambo in Mbeli and Ekaso, Bambala, Ayeye, Eyonga, Melimbikani, Soomboo and Ngbanda in Yandoumbe for sharing with us both their extraordinary knowledge of the forest as well as their music. Thank you also to Angela, Lyndsay and Thomas for their kind hospitality in Mbeli and also to Fafa, our camp manager, for looking after us so well. I would like to express my gratitude to Saira Robertson of the Cameroon Wildlife Aid Foundation for introducing us to the orphan gorillas at the sanctuary in Cameroon. Uli Braun of the World Wide Fund for Nature in the Central African Republic was a star. He not only helped us greatly during our stay, coming to our rescue when our vehicle got stuck, but also provided us with some valuable insights into the region. Thank you also to the Sous-prefet of Bayanga for his warm welcome to C.A.R. It was a great pleasure to meet Chloe and the other researchers at Bai Hoku and I'd like to say a how grateful I am to you for taking us to meet the magnificent Mlima and the other gorillas. Andrea Turkalo is one of the most dedicated field researchers I've met and I can't thank her enough for making us feel so at home in her camp at Dzanga *bai*, introducing us to the elephants, giving me her comments on relevant sections of this book and not least, for being there for me with Matofi, when I was charged by an elephant. In addition to Matofi, I would like to express my deepest thanks to Melebu, Banda and Sa'konga for being such skilled trackers. I would also like to say a special thank you to Louis Sarno for inviting us to Yandoumbe and giving us a privileged insight into Ba'aka culture.

My parents have, as always, been fantastic and I can't thank them enough for both their moral support and thoughts on the manuscript. Thank you also to my sisters, Francine and Marijke, and the many friends who have been so encouraging and helpful. In particular, I would like to thank Mike Scott, who once again played vital role in technological support and also John Coward, Carlton Ramone, Dan Elston, and Sibs and Gabriel Gbadamosi for being so patient with me when I was feeling frazzled. Many thanks also to Justin Avery and Jonnie Keeling for helping to proof read the manuscript. Most of all I want to thank my beloved Dan Rees for being there for me, giving me so many valuable comments on the manuscript, proof reading chapters and helping me keep things in perspective.

Finally, I would like to express my deepest gratitude to Caroline Taggart for her excellent editorial advice on the manuscript and to Rupert Lancaster at Hodder & Stoughton who has been so supportive throughout. Last but not least, I would like to say a heartfelt thank you to my wonderful agent, Sheila Ableman, without whom this book would not have been written.

Picture Acknowledgements

James Aldred: page 6 (top); page 7 (inset); page 18 (bottom); page 20 (bottom). Jake Drake-Brockman: page 5 (top); page 14 (bottom left); page 15; page 18 (top); page 19; page 20 (top); page 21; page 22 (top); page 23 (bottom). Mark Flowers: page 9; page 13 (bottom). Cede Prudente: page 2 (top); page 6 (bottom). Simon Wagen: page 1; page 2 (bottom); page 3; page 4 (top); page 5 (bottom); page 7; page 8; page 10-11; page 12 (top); page 13 (top); page 13 (bottom right); page 15; page 16; page 21 (top); page 22.

We do hope that you have enjoyed reading this large print book.

Did you know that all of our titles are available for purchase?

We publish a wide range of high quality large print books including:
Romances, Mysteries, Classics
General Fiction
Non Fiction and Westerns

Special interest titles available in large print are:
The Little Oxford Dictionary
Music Book
Song Book
Hymn Book
Service Book

Also available from us courtesy of Oxford University Press:
Young Readers' Dictionary
(large print edition)
Young Readers' Thesaurus
(large print edition)

For further information or a free brochure, please contact us at:
Ulverscroft Large Print Books Ltd.,
The Green, Bradgate Road, Anstey,
Leicester, LE7 7FU, England.
Tel: (00 44) 0116 236 4325
Fax: (00 44) 0116 234 0205